Only Fig & Prosciutto

Luke Whitington

Only Fig & Prosciutto
New & Collected Poems

To my mother and daughter

Only Fig & Prosciutto: New & Collected Poems
ISBN 978 1 76041 313 2
Copyright © text Luke Whitington 2017
Cover design: Julian Canny

First published 2017 by
GINNINDERRA PRESS
PO Box 3461 Port Adelaide 5015 Australia
www.ginninderrapress.com.au

Contents

I	Italy	9
	Venus in Rome	11
	Only fig, wine and prosciutto	12
	Cappuccino and almond cake	14
	A nostalgic stroll in Venice	16
	Antipasto Orazio	18
	Antony at the window	19
	Bells can remember	20
	Bologna	22
	Caravaggio	24
	Chiaroscuro	25
	Firenze	26
	Firenze, thunder over Cosimo	29
	Grand Duke – Tuscany on a Florentine horse	31
	Headless goddess in Naples	33
	His words haunt the ancient hills	37
	Italian singer girl	40
	Love and shattered marble	42
	Mona on the other side	44
	Pay back	45
	Piazza delle Signoria; the square of the lords	47
	Polgeto, a village of Umbria	48
	Ravello – south from Naples	50
	Rita, naked in the sunflowers	52
	Roma dawning	53
	Ruins	55
	Sarina at Santo Stefano	57
	Siena	59
	The fig	60
	The last lunch	61
	The Loggia, Piazza delle Signoria	63

The man in the Academia	64
The moon, the tower and the manuscript	67
The Naked Lunch	70
The swallows in Saint Peters Square	72
Tivoli	73
Torte al testo	75
Umbrian moon	77
Venetian palazzo	79
Venice, summer ends	81
Brodsky	83

II Elsewhere — 87

Expatriate	89
In memory of Basil	91
Postcard from Latvia	92
Rovigno; the beautiful banker	94
Praying aloud	96
A candle in the window	97
A lull in the afternoon	99
Abbeville	100
Achilles	103
After Akhmatova	104
Berryman's island	105
Broken chandelier	107
Central park and Columbus Avenue	109
Fear of life?	112
Five seasons at Portlick (all in one day)	113
Gull Man	114
Heaney's wind	116
Ikos then	117
Ikos	119
Lost realms	121
Orderly encumbrances	125

Portlick Castle	125
Return to the west	129
Remember Anektoria	131
Rilke's Torso	132
Syros	133
The Bog at Clonmacnoise	134
The Dead Poet	137
Dust and time	139
No door to a stone	140
The waves tell them	141
Syros and the last sunset	144

III Love and other trouble — 147

Nardia	149
Aphrodite?	150
Swallows inside	151
A bumpkin heart	152
And love of hide and seek	154
Apricots and cumquats	155
Injuries	157
Love not the wind	158
Lunch in Napoli	159
My Daisy Mae	161
Nine lives	163
Reunion at the remembered lake	164
Rodin	166
The heavenly tie	167
The swimmers	169
Woman Cat	170
Tania	171

IV Mongarlowe Country — 173

A human weathervane	175
Her coiled blue curves	176

Southbound	178
The rock pool	180
A chair, best company?	182
A cliff of sky between the birds	184
A friend, called mother	186
Acres of sunset	188
A single red rose	189
Sky rider	190
Dawn bird	191
Dawn walk at Mongarlowe	193
Fido	195
For whom?	196
Indian summer	197
Mother again	198
Nature sinuous with her maker	200
Not taken	203
Omelette?	205
One bird	206
Playful thinking	207
The last cull on the place	208
The man without leaves	213
The marathon	215
The mountains watch	216
The old place	219
Those moments	221
Peninsula	222
Washing up	223
Will I?	224
Towards another summer	225
Acknowledgements	227

I
Italy

Venus in Rome

We met in the ruins
Of someone else's civilisation

Under a dying warrior
You offered me a torn half of your sandwich

Around us the silent industry
Of thighs, calves, spears

And discus-throwing arms
Held their swaying moment.

A god, legless, armless, headless
Alive in absences, a plank of debris

Tossed up from art's wreckage –
Once smooth curve of space

Today our staid facsimile.
Your eyes, sight for a divine statue

Thighs lithe on the heavy bench
Would find ample employment here

Lighter amongst the sobering myths
Moving through the crowd of legends.

I'll walk you home, I said. Where is it?

Near the Pantheon, you said. I live
Perched high up, with the pigeons…

In the dim twilight of the room
A glimmer in her eyes spoke of Venus.

Only fig, wine and prosciutto

In the gilded mirror we sit – expectant
Yet distracted, sallow figures in the glow
Of a hotel dining room – the hush of luxury
Hovers in the background, waiters blur
Passing with tinklings of glasses and silver.

Thoughts of finished love-making; touches hover
And float away, words start to form
Lips but vanish into softer, vaguer notions
Our limbs begin to wake, stirring from luxurious slumber –

Dazed we contemplate a pyramid of bruise-purple figs
All painterly perfect – some peeled to a ribbed green
Some split wide open, inviting the tongue and lips to try

To taste them with each silky slice of Parma ham
Folded in ripples of cream and redness across our plates.
Under its dark blue skin, an unpeeled fig waits
For our palate, with its last pulp of honey-slow flavour –

And your smile broadens as I watch
You stab your fork into a pink slice of prosciutto
As you anticipate the flavour of rosy flesh
Your eyes swimming with reflected light

Swirling up from rubescent wine from Umbria, Torregiano –
A Terroir type, grapes trellised and grown and plucked
Carried in baskets from the tilled earth of their hilly province.
Your nose crinkles – another sniff of tannin pungency
Cured ham and fig and wine nurtured from ochre *chernozem*

Chewed and tippled carefully, warm and cool from a fecund earth
A quick taste; a quiver to the heart, masticated in recollection
Of summer and winter harvesting, feasts and slanting memories
Begin to mingle, tumbling, fusing in my mouth –

Crisp combines with soft and also effervescence
Seconds later, lush and lean slipping down
A sumptuous buttering, a plump delight
Remaining on the tongue, more wine – now

Intoxicating us – draining us down – the tipsy ruler of our minds.

Cappuccino and almond cake

The past is never past
Floating in some rear-view mirror
Or sticky right there on the tip of your tongue –
Now it wobbles in a glass before my eyes
Or is under my hand or a folded napkin
Lingering, glowing, shining elsewhere

In many things – a glass of milk, a circling whiff of wine –
Famously, in a provincial Frenchman's little biscuit.
Today I nibble an Italian almond biscuit
A Tuscan vineyard is there in the raisin
An almond crumbling is like the *faux* resistance

Of your fingers; curling expectant on damask linen
Or absently stroking moist cotton, textures I remember
Touching – like the slow imprint of your kisses
The taste of lips, blackberry-burnished, ripened
From drinking country wine; summer drowsing thoughts
Vapour-drenched memory; I sip again the curve of your thigh

Under damp fabric; twisted torsos; tongues
Swimming in the milk of lust and kindness and
Strangeness; saliva a sweet elixir in crowded mouths –
Who said the past is dead? I wipe my brow
The scent of memory lingers, makes a pale stain on my napkin

And my cup chatters back into its saucer.
In the little porthole of drained froth
Creamy streaks show my fortune has been told;
Moments to happen soon, circle in frothy caramels
A future swirled from random circumstances; scents

And flavours and textures – promising light and shade in a life.

A nostalgic stroll in Venice

The noise of history
Has left the sky, this evening
This walk – time is now water
Light is inventing higher realms

The gondolas pass sliding dark bellies
Over supple little waves
Talk bursts from your mouth;
Exile and guide – a guide to exile?

Bilingual words issue like fish –
The scales of a curving canal-fish
Alongside slide away in diagonals
The elements drift in sensual ecstasy

Sky in redness, air in readiness
Reflections erotic, promiscuous –
We walk on, visiting unlit churches
Rubbing the plaques of the great dead

Smiling at cats as if they were old friends
Talking of what people may have meant
Remembering cafes, bars in old towns
That drift in the browns of the past.

It is almost dawn! The waves still
Move – bearing depths of darkness
Catching the sun's glow sloping into a long stare
The water is changing; a chameleon mirror

Flirting with towers of heavens, throwing light
Into the arches, deeper into the darkest interiors.
Marble, stone, glimpses of bronze
Shudder and shift in reflections;

Elements in love – a luminous chattering –
Witnessing bystanders; cartwheeling arches
And stone squares at the edges, pretending to be water
Pretending to be fluid, amorphous; free like time.

Antipasto Orazio

Pick up the little loaf
And tear off the end of it –
I'll pour the wine with a measuring hand
Let's taste the crust and marrow, the freshness of today

Break it before you raise your glass with mine –
And let us toast a Roman poet
Who in all his doubt, always
Knew when and how to praise

The virtue of the living moment –
First sipping it, then relishing it, until
It falls back to just below the rim. Now let's pick
Up our forks and knives and begin

To explore the assortment of flavours
The succulence and abundance
The languid sense of sublimity
In savouring what we are generously given.

Antony at the window

You believed in the gods
But Dionysus had not noticed
You slumped at the window
You watched

The midnight procession –

Human and hollow gutted
You put on your mask
Of invincibility, immortal again
You waved from the window

As an erect Emperor God
Would do to his followers
Who did not think to look up
Clanking onwards to the dawn in the east

Already mourning their losses.

Bells can remember

A different, strident sound today
Exuberant and echoing
Like rising hearts of waves, blazing.
Years ago behind the Venetian fog
I hoped there were angels, hovering there
Behind dull, muffled December days

The sun vagrant behind vague
Outlines of towers and domes;
Contemplative profiles in that soup of grey air
Lights in windows over canals
Seemed to be floating lanterns
Leading, intriguing me on – here I walked where

He had walked along his tidemarks

But never crossed him; I with my poet's cloak
Black Sicilian sombrero, tapping
My unconvinced cane – where he had scurried
In his old raincoat and indifferent cap, scavenging
For words – the depth of hollowness in the fog
Did not echo but the stones endured a new poem

As I muttered it under my breath – over and over.
I dread to think if he had ever heard me
And reversed his tracks down another alley
Escaping my ongoing, doddering meter.
Today a vastly different light, a sluggish mood of evening sky
And I walk through shadows of my old self

Plainly dressed now as mister nobody-knows man
Without a Borselino hat or cloak to climb the steps of the Rialto
There in any old shirt, I remember his musing
About foggy Venice in winter;
'Like Greta Garbo on her side, swimming.'
Even though spring has almost thawed

I won't follow her sidestroke, naked or clothed
Diving below to reach for her in the streams of blue cold.

Bologna

Lord I am golden from drinking
Your famous Lambrusco
I've stared deep into all of your saints'
Eyes; gorgeous Cecilia, modest Mary Magdalen
Trailing threads of gold through their dresses;
The master Raphael painted, wondering blasphemously
If they were pink or golden on the other side.

Under slow golden light, under the arches
We ate tortellini, once fashioned after
The curls in a courtesans' navel, spied through a tavern keyhole
And made by the chef, a mesmerised voyeur –
From butter, oil, eggs, flour and water…

Now descending navels move about, creamily in my mouth
And my mind's lascivious tongue slips over the curve of a belly
Down to a lower unbuttoning of life
I imagine I'm lying with her on the edge of the bed
Knowing the hungry eye watches, blinking lust through a keyhole.

Now some of the sweet and nutty Parma ham
Streaked with creamy ribbons of fat
Draped over split purple figs
Covering their luscious ruby insides…
And cream spiced with truffles and Grana Padano
Slides in yellows over my tagliatelle –
I lift the strands, wrapped round my fork
As I anticipate, sniffing life's pungent source.

My tongue swims on through voluptuous textures
As I juggle a last prayer to Mary and Altissima Cecilia
And also to our *carissimo* friend, Master Raphael;
Please forgive me, Maestro, for my ordinary images
Of what you have already made magnificently famous…

Forgive me as well dear lord, my gastric promiscuity
Swallowing this platter of Emilian tortellini
Under your saintly alabaster gaze, under
Your patronage, under the drunken towers of our beloved Bologna.

Caravaggio

You can come up from the cold basement
Caravaggio – the Pope has pardoned you
For a truckload of chiaroscuros – now those dramatic
Blood-red backdrops do not need to hide –
Those faces of torment; half dead, half alive
Will – adorning his corridors – stop his weary eye.

Master of bizarre moments; trifectas of love, avarice and cruelty
Innocence in turgid silence before its murderer
Smouldering moods, death in dripping shadows; now
Free again to walk the calamitous streets
Of the Papal city; under her domes her towers
Returning back to the gaping, echoing mouth of the Pantheon.

Free again to dart, spin about, to pick any old fight
Free to delight in the cities' rambling
Sprawling insanity; walking arms outstretched
In a trance with death and life; befriending tarts, beggars
Thieves, a homeless friend, with daggers hung from both hands

Looking into faces of the oppressed
The fierce life; half nascent, half massacred there –
Walking toward the future duel, the relished fight
Toward the highest or lowest – ranked enemy
The next conflicted, stage-lit, depicted destiny –
The brush, palette, and rage of a cornered, crouched life.

Chiaroscuro

Is this the name for a condition?
The one no one chooses to talk about
You're all sitting around my bedside
And no one is getting the point.

I prefer twisted shadows
To what has happened to my face
I am fighting to calm two halves
One dark, ironic; the other of innocent light.

I clutch my warring cheeks
The history of art
Can truly stuff itself
I want nothing more to take place

In my regard – don't even mention me
No glory or redemption, no fall, no rise
Nothing spectacular, just give my one face back
My calm, my perspective, my angle

Please – and both eyes identical.
Get back to your brush and palette, Caravaggio
And it's either going to be light or dark
I am tired of juggling both

Give me one shade, one restful colour
Not this half of that one
And half of the other one
This farce of one or the other

This schizophrenic duelling as drama!

Firenze

The gold on this door is thin
But you cannot break it
No matter how much you beat it –
Like the iron ring of the will – it will
Not disappear, remaining
Thin – but always obdurate.

Il Duomo, with a *sospiro* to Dante.

Your shadow falls
Beside mine
While we are arguing
Over coffee or ice cream –
Both will do it seems – and each shadow finds
The time to lengthen
Legs linking, outlines agreeing, coinciding.

Santa Croce, with an *occhio* toward Dante.

Our shadows turn
To go back
The way we came
We accept their persuasion
More in disagreement
But resigned we step
Quickly, into a rhythm of strident agreement.

Santo Spirito with a *pensierino* for Dante.

Having listened
To the doves' warbled
Lessons in philosophy –
We sit on carved benches and stare across stones
And listen in to our own shadows
Those dark outlines
That spoke hours before
In brighter tones of conversation.

The old bridge, water *torbida* with ancient names.

They all stood here
And must have leant over
Making a wish
Or even knowing it was already granted…

Dreams unfulfilled, remembering innocence or ill-gotten
   things, memories
Of love and good or bad luck – betrayals flowing away
In time – and Cellini, perched like a rudder man on this
   pedestal
Is our silent offsider. Before him poets, emperors
And vagabonds – scruffy or elegant, lost or rediscovered
Must have stared at the waters and wondered
On so much time passed already, quietly
Descending, woven, dovetailed under all the bridges

To tumble closer, swelling up and down under this bridge –
A swirling place and above the structure of arches, the only throughway
To get past the arching shops, with their diamonds, rings and chains of gold
And all the shadows crawling slowly along; behind or before their owners
Shapes of lovers and adulterers, children or adults, some wicked and some innocent
Shadows of souls come from nowhere, with nowhere to hide –
Either lighter or darker – steps and thoughts edging ahead under the poet's sky.

i.m. Dante Alighieri, who inspired many to visit these places

Firenze, thunder over Cosimo

Over the Square of the Lords the autumn sky
Battles with light and dark
Serrated by stonework the stormy apricot clouds
Muster and gallop, plume and prance

The ranks of walls stand fast in varied angles
Soaring toward the geometric porthole in the sky
And Cosimo surveys his options from his bronze
Warrior horse, as light fleeing the skies

Like swallows – scatters across the sea of stones.
The deserted square waits for the deluge.
Moderately safe under my café umbrella
With the wind rippling in the canvas I sip on my Chianti

Trying new blood – *sangue nero*, for my tongue
Savouring massacres – of love, trust, loyalty and saintliness –
Judith poised with her sacred sword – frozen for
The second brutal stroke, the mighty tyrant
Risen from his bed, bleeding, too weak to plead for forgiveness.

The pigeons swoop again through the turbulent air
Intoxicated with the elements, preparing themselves
For clash and fusion they veer and swerve
Alongside the colonnades, past the bulging walls
Of the fortress tower, spiral over the triumphant fans of arches

And peel away like fragments of disintegrating stone
And flying rubble – then looping into a wide arc they turn and swoop
Again, down to the loggia as if to a heavenly conductor's baton –
To perch on the shoulders and heads of legendary

Victims, tyrants and bloody-minded monsters –
Unperturbed about murder or pillage or slaughter
They descend on the pinnacle of rape, or on the raised avenging sword
Or on the mane of a guardian lion, fluttering amongst

The best and the worse for seconds in an epoch before they settle
And huddle not unlike myself under my creaking umbrella.
And we – the grey birds and I, wait for the first crack
The echoing zigzag of light, all stillness in the soundlessness

Of bells and the clouds descending to smother, enclose the frozen horse and rider.

Grand Duke – Tuscany on a Florentine horse

A storm begins – dark clouds roll over
The pondering tower – below the bronze duke
Rides his steed into rumpled lilac light
Stern building rise into the changing light

Snagging on walls – time drenched layers of ochre stone
The square still stands at attention
But nothing will happen again –
The history of the ruled and their rulers
And their artists is over – the Renaissance

Is spent and breathless at the finishing line in this piazza.
In benign or tortured shapes the statues left
Replace the words, the conversations, the written tomes
The manuscripts – the crimes of passion, the cold dagger's
    thrust
From the crowd, the deft curves from a master's hands

The perfect attitudes of madness or death sliding away
Downward before our eyes, hopes always shattered – is what
    is left in this place
Sublimely, uncannily interpreted; almost an archive of
    rationalised violence
Assembled here under one loggia – in a shadowy reminder of
    a harsher light of history.

And you wonder why, draining your last glass of Chianti –
    we ever questioned
Our mortal wickedness – the capacity to murder rape and lay
    waste
In the name of wisdom, conquest, religion and orderly,
    decent containment
Always insatiable – sanctified by the great sculptors, in
    exquisite works of art.

Headless goddess in Naples

Her head is forgotten, her former gaze
Absorbed by sand, clay, pebbles –
A critical absence stares through layers
Of misplaced time – up to a spectre of an idea.

However a navel is left there for us – the button pinned
On the curve of her stomach –
A neat distraction, a knot to an unknown ending –
A send off present from her Homeric birthing…
Yes, all of that and if it doesn't work – a convenient orifice for a pearl or a sapphire.

But on this afternoon a few thousand years after – it will be another kind –
Another form of an eye that mimes for the missing mouth
That tells just as much for an absent smile
That sees right through an empire's groaning secrets…
You might try to imagine – closing both eyes tightly –

The navel reminding you it had been revealed again
To refresh memory of many undulations of a life
Launched once, into raunchy dips, from side to side
As those golden hips and conquering thighs swayed their way through the world

Of gods and goddesses' business; heavenly wars and soaring stars' prophecies
Summoning several contrivances – to disturb our fate –
An unintended oracle, a quick twist to our beginnings and endings.
Above all, this orifice had got up to several tricks – to seduce minds
And sooth and beguile flesh – it was not required to devise a way of foreseeing things –

Was even good enough just to be pretty – a nice turn – like an eyebrow arched
Over a secret – or like lips curled around an intriguing question –
And was never intended to be a soothsayer, or an honorary oracle either –
And blindly stare through one spiralling epitaph forever, left

As a porthole for a headless, expressionless life…
Now try to forget the missing eyes, the nose, the chin and the throat
Gone to their heavenly absence – look at the nipples –
Sense how they might protrude, penetrate, even kiss
The pout inside your mind – see the curve of the belly –

See how it brushes slowly across your lips – moistening your
    imagining
Igniting your senses, searing across your future tense –
And feel the fingers as they slide blindly over your lips –
With slowed heartbeats, feel the buttocks plush against your
    palms
You have it all – enough in spades to fulfil all your requisites,
    all the big ticks for love –
The absence of a head, eyes, smile only persuades your heart
    to grow fonder –

Now you know – I believe – I should really like to do it – the
    idea warming
Nicely – although really I'm not in a position to take her
    home –
And if I could somehow haul her – lug her whole thwarted
    loveliness
Out to the car park…but it still wouldn't work; I don't
Have a car boot or a passenger door big enough –

To try to stuff in the drama; those swan-curved legs, the
    hesitant arm, the durable breasts
And all the other missing bits…and what if I returned home
    one day and I kissed her –
And found her lips still warm? And what, if like Pygmalion,
    I tried
To make a child; my only issue, spawned from those marble
    thighs?

And it goes on and on – until when she cracked apart
With passion – would her last arm crush me to death?
In our single mortal embrace? Her breasts
Still curved murderously against my nose –

As I died for love, moaning fidelity for the first time… No…

I must not join that coterie; centuries of dreaming sculptors
The bard himself and the modern playwrights – the lonely
    poets, even some pop singers –
There will be no *Winter's Tale* – awakened by this – she – a so
    sensitively sculptured
Creature – now I see her navel is only sweet debris – a coiled
    shell –

A relic of a Virgin's wish – and her sigh that never had time
To soften – her final place
Should remain here in this museum room –
Those lineaments poised before a bronze glow forever

Her fingers counting leaves on some celestial pond
Glimmering in the future – floating under farewelling clouds
Turning around in time, turning for always, always –
Her navel the last remembered spinning orifice –
A recurring impression; a golden moment, long gone.

His words haunt the ancient hills

'Oh spring of Bandusiae, more splendid than glass' – Horace, Ode 3.13

You know it from before but touch again the cold of dry clad stone
In sunken cellar rooms, dim light hibernating, secure from the downpour
Of Italian sunlight; waiting moments, drips of silence, and when
You reluctantly come outside; the light cascades and rocks your senses

And you hear his words come light and whispering
Through nearby olives, flocks of silver leaves and swaying branches
While you watch the cypresses on the hill, flex, whip and wobble in the wind
And see the clouds left in streaks to make one great arch across a backdrop

Of oak forests – greenness gathering down the hillsides – and at the last crest
Shadows falling from trees into a fermenting haze;
Columns of light slide across the lake like a forgotten element
Of wind – and you know from the battered book in your pocket
The Roman poet Horace strolled here – often down these groves

Now let go, unkempt – orderly plantations and staged
    cypresses
Strayed into a ragged park, once a farming Eden
For centuries; and the poet would stop for a pause on this
    natural terrace
And pensively smell or chew a random olive leaf
To savour better an inner sense of this place; its lazy peace
Under drowsing shadows, falling in cloaks higher over the
    Sabine mountains.

Doves warble in the background, the air distilled after
    morning rain
Views brittle as perception, hem a clarity around you –
There, not far from your feet, are twisted trunks
Of ancient olive trees plunged into dark brown earth
Swaying arms over sparsely grassed, stone-speckled hillsides…

And you know from the words weighing in your pocket
The gods and fauns of hills, woods, valleys and fields wafted
    here, a further
Existence ago; once as free and light as these dustless currents
    of air
And the Roman poet surely felt their presence here

As he walked these groves during the hours of slow siestas –
A timelessness disturbed by the faintest sounds of bells,
   approaching and gone
A place to sense the impact of a moment's brush as it comes
   and goes…
And then as you hear that sound again, looking through the
   interwoven branches

You can see suddenly a flock of sheep – right above – a line
   leaping
In clumps of whiteness, arching across the belly of blue sky –
And you hear those thoughts he wrote down afterwards,
   streaming
Across pages of his life, flickering through the lazy summers
Azure melting blues into odes; words riding vagabond, deep
   in your pocket.

Italian singer girl

And the leaves spun
Their innocuous dance about the grave
In the grove opening deep into the forest
And the music played in the wind

As if a madman's feet, not a fiddlers' – danced about there
Amongst leaves emigrating around and past the fresh-filled mound
Across the sunlight sailing through in little ships of grass –
The dancer with no shadow – later you grew to know

It was death celebrating its harvest
But as a young man you only remember her lovely face
Drifting slowly like a kite and vanishing into pale pink light
Rising to a single glint curling in the sky – today wherever you are

In whatever dialect of whichever borrowed land, whatever season of the eagle
The swallow, sparrow or the crow, travelling with shadows of clouds, the colours
Of spring, winter or autumn, or reaching up for the blinding ropes of summer sunlight –
The bird with a face rises into the lightness of bright haze or slower, auburn colours.

Death did not take her from your heart, death stamped around
Furiously anchoring its tenure – the sodden winter ground below
That took her under – and as you watch the whimsical language
Of wind in love with a leaf now and a leaf
Chasing the wind's tail around, around and around – then you remember

How the leaves became silence
And for years remained so and how human sounds
Came and went, minstrels of backgrounds you passed as that nomad –
That strange stranger as you skirted around, around always
And the sound of silence in the sky of leaves
Forever reminds you of the fiddlers that day

Playing for her memory as the madman – death – skipped
And leaped but could not reach one leaf
To catch the sense of her – now like a leaf descending, she
Is turning, turning, to land in a touch
A finger's touch, light as one leaf on the top of your head.

Love and shattered marble

Breakfast for dinner and lunch for dawn
Disorientated again; time a wheel rolling along
Careering this way and that way –
Lying in bed giddy, slack from lovemaking

Looking at light; its gentlest sheen, its wax intrigued with
    your skin
Infused over your belly, breasts, and the sabre of one raised
    thigh.
Your spine is one of the contours of sensual time – it curves
To places I have known, come to and gone from, retraced

And returned – often in search of an unclear self
And perhaps also an unclear notion; a pilgrim following
Fumbling songs of loss – hate, forgiveness and thankfully
    some love.
Lovemaking is our brief moment of magic
Become the pay-off for being so quaintly mortal –

Flashes of the immortal flicker in the sexual cry
To a higher kingdom; corner of some exalted sky –
Watching you as your limbs tremble
With a rush of remembering and forgetting breath

And I think of the goddesses of Rome who could not flee
Those loping barbarians; black minds rummaging through
    smoke
And rubble, sacking anything and smashing walls of history –
Goddesses heaved and hauled away, dragged and
Dumped headless from a cart, then broken up and burnt into
    lumps of lime.

Loveliness pulverised into mortar or fertiliser
Into top-dressing for fields where bearded, northern gods ruled.
I reach across and touch just to make sure again
Of the curve of your breast, your eyelids glistening through
   wet hair –

All still there; a goddess breathing steadily, safe or unsafe in
   my care.

Mona on the other side

The smile knows something more –
Is there another moment in her mind's eye?
Another landscape, another dusk, perhaps another lover

On the other side; shoulders of a painting press back onto
　　hers –
The past a darker, elusive work of art
A slow dance – but how long past? How far off?

Ten minutes? One hour? Half a life, even time
She did not dare to live – or is it just her again
Recurring there in a captured second of recollection –

The same enigmatic expression
On the other side, the same cypresses
Rising to the crest of her rose-soft consciousness –

The same Tuscany; noble, proud, her mother hills of home –
An inland oasis of the renaissance; and there she is
Again, almost the same beautiful creature; an eligible

Comely Tuscan maiden, dressed in her Sunday best, staring
　　blithely out
From her birthright into the future – and then the frame
Spins around and stops – to the same portrait with her
　　tongue poked out!

Pay back

One day, I swear, I'll do you, Venus
Marinated in your turmoil, juices, sinews
Hips, reduced, roasted to a slow perfection

Then chew you slowly up for having made me wait
In hopelessness for all these years
Lingering in dim museum rooms

For at least a blink, a flicker of some emotion
And all I got for my worry was the subliminal –
Those unlockable thighs, that frozen pose, of someone
Who was supposed to be – the goddess of love?

In afternoons of raining sunshine, I paid as I always did for my ticket
And ventured into one more room where they kept you –
Always waiting for a sign, I touched your immovable

Fingers, I brushed your frigid lips with blood-warmed fingers
Nothing shivered, came unstuck, or flinched to my touch
You were enclosed forever in your lycra of skin-tight-white marble –

Even your navel was a beautiful fake, no trembling there – what despair
For a romantic bloke; armless follower of gods, oracles and legends –
I knew from stories of ancient history, barbarians baked statues down to lime

When they carted away half of Rome; Art desecrated into fertiliser
And sorry but good riddance my dear, for the years waiting for one pale smile –
So my sweetheart, curvaceous or not, it looks like a roast crackling and dripping

For both of us – especially for you my love, tonight – either
That or I'm going to have to find a very cold chisel
And try for the last time, to hammer, to chip, to inch

In deeper again – for some momentary emotion – if only the slightest quiver of you.

Piazza delle Signoria; the square of the lords

Giambologna's rape of the Sabine women –
Much too beautiful – to introduce terror…
The launched symmetry, the woman

Suspended effortlessly above two men
Like a turning threesome; a circling team
Of Immortals – leaping into historical basketball.

A moment of nurtured stone, asserting
Marble is lighter than air, the sphere higher up
A figment of imagination, a resonance

You are meant to watch, later in recollection –
While her buttocks balance on the thrust of
A perpendicular line of male sinews and muscles…

Every time you cross the piazza, passing
The corner of the tower – rising stones like a prow
Cutting the light in half, you like to see

The same pigeon there, using Cosimo Medici's
Head as a lookout, a belvedere, the master
Of his steed and the Renaissance

Wears his fringe of dried excrement, undistracted
Urging his horse further into the history of cash and art.
And across in the shadows of the loggia

The three figures continue to leap
Like a fountain of flesh in joyous liberated stone –
Marble recurring in a fountain of ecstasy

Three leaps at a time in a pigeon's wing beat of memory.

Polgeto, a village of Umbria

'The same landscape always repeated' – Vittorio Sereni

Thinking of the lazy green river
The watching hills, you revisit the Tiber valley
Village perched halfway up its sharpest mountain
The tenuous inhabitants called Contadini –
Cultivators – who live in a world above bubbles of traffic.

Quietness measured by the ticking
Of the hoe and mattock; the snips of pruning shears –
People with a knack for poverty, skilled in unprofitable
Schemes of seasons and weather, knowing by heart
The accords and discords, the inward song of weather-worship

Minds and bodies geared to survival, meticulous
In few choices – seed cast in spring, grain snatched in summer
Harvest; always-ancient song, and winter months of watching
A landscape resting, while the wind seethes and bellows
To itself – and shadows move as they do through leafless
　grassless places.

Above the indifferent river of traffic exists a realm, a religion
　of doing without
Priests might only witness or whisper a tribute about –
And yet they were well fed on it; clearest eyes, shining hair
Movements supple and brisk, melodic shouting
Shuddering welcomes, a big hint of curiosity

In knowing smiles and their only treasure, or vice, even, was food
Celebrated and shared, with anyone, in frockless, ordained austerity.
So today in my own landscape I see their faces, nut brown
In whatever month; returning from vineyards or descending the olive groves
Their plain secret, poverty – filling those harvest sacks – and my astonishment

At the ongoing practise of a worn, well-grooved simplicity
Their boisterous acceptance of their lot; people from another time
Living above the traffic of ours, living for a different god
A god in a cob of corn, a god in a sack of wheat, a god in a glass
Of glinting wine – and remembered in my own shadowy wind

Trembling through feeble sunshine; memory climbing north
Through orderly fields and forests festive with light
The winding road equally eager to get there
As I drive my car higher into their sparkling spring
And I read their lofty, poppy-dotted fields and meadows
With an acute eye, borrowed from poverty; in years of auburn exile.

Ravello – south from Naples

The terrace of infinity
The belvedere of the infinite.
The parasol pines twist and leap like dancers
Or hover with wings of clumped needles.

Rivers of moments
Light falling through green
Fragments of a summer
Are receding in your smile –

The delight of your resolve
Under the sun, is harsh as light –
Cruel like your eyes as they glitter into future adultery.
I watch their gaze into some distant future

Leaving our bundle of moments
Wedged under a shadow
That shakes itself and settles with branches
To cover the unwanted, second-hand secret.

The olive shifts with soft creaks, sailing
Now with the wind, the uppermost tendrils –
The topmost leaves, flow west; the easterly is in your head
Streaming toward the sun and its heavy certainty –

Sinking, easing now, into the vulnerable curve of the sea.
I look at a sadness of ebbing golden water –
This sea of sirens I had come with you a long way to see
The apricots, crimsons and bloods, seeping

Across to the waiting rocks below; dark, hunched creatures
Caught stepping down into the flow of an ending
As our fingers let go, awkward with a certain uncertainty
And you turn to part, stepping down the geranium-petalled path

Past the pedestals and the busts of sun-reddened emperors and courtesans.
Your skirts sway, your step is lighter, married to another place and measure.
Your silhouette is like shapely driftwood – remembered in the darkening traffic of light.

Rita, naked in the sunflowers

She said in the early morning
The sunflowers kept her awake
She watched them watching us

Through the night, those massive eyes
Surreal and sad in the moonlight
She said I said they tried to speak

In my dream and wanted to save me
But I couldn't keep myself awake
And I flopped back down beside her and drowned

Arm over arm in a yellow sea of sunflowers –
Great ochre eyes kept floating through the moonlit window…

Today I see her, years after, still there on the hill
Picking the random poppies as she steps
Carefully down through the turning-all-seeing stamen

Her shoulders and hips bared to the light
Curved yokes for the weight of unashamed sunshine
Hair tossed into a halo, into its buoyant chaos of yellow.

Roma dawning

Startled at dawn
By your languorous slow-pink-toned body
A landscape turned onto one side
And not, in the half light, yet quite

Believable; in darkness can a sleeping man and woman
Become one continuous island? How did I, did we, get here?
You in your dusk-coloured sleep seem ancient
Something that has always been –
I am like a new set of hills pushed up
From the subterranean music of the earth;

Nervous, uncertain, concerned
I contemplate touching you
But that right now, would be imperfect –
Your breath is magnificent enough
Like dreamed bells shuddering
And I restrain myself
I do not disturb the dawning cathedral of your being.

There is a rickety bridge which links
Our dreams; mine sluggish, swinging half awake, yours
Febrile, taut like a tongue of rope; the light is growing
Around your shape, my eyes delight in its rose-tinged glow –
Where is Knidos, my Greek goddess?
Is she close, here, growing into life inside you?

Outside in the ancient, loaf paved square the air tumbles with
   bells
The endless cycle, the millennium turning of sound
To accompany star-flecked heavens in one arching journey;
The domes murmuring a day of rest, a pause in the transit
Of all breath, tolling instants, while my hand rests
On your hip and waits; fingertips attentive to your breathing
Ready to continue the night's journey – feeling a way along
   the swaying bridge.

Ruins

The temple has fallen
In love with the grass
Curved sections, half
Obscured, hint at more
The whipping grass will tell no more

The glint in long running grass blades
Shares nothing; except the wind –
At this café table, cheese and olive
Taste different, in southern Sicily

The sheep's breath is still there, shared
With every olive's green bitterness
And enlivens the tongue, the crumbling
Substance of cave-aged cheese

Is a foil for an olive's ripe discordancy.
Wine, black, smeared
Like youth's blood on your tongue and lips;
Peeling back to a smile – guileful and demonic –

The sun our padrone – our straw-hatted gatekeeper
Lord of a sultry, pagan world.
The grass swishes
Over the fallen Doric column
A long thigh undressed by the wind

Our hands flirt under the table
The sky is benign, watching us, slyly
While fingers play ambitious roles
Moistened from a long time ago –

More games are remembered between touches.

But today with you the swallows
Seem more alive, devilish even
As they turn chasing shadows of gods
Through the columns, in and out; light and dark of an epoch –

Last night we watched them rise and flourish at midnight
From shallow waters, gold dripping from our thighs
You splashed your cheeks with the gorgeous wetness
And drops ran down, molten between your breasts

For seconds I saw the rocks, following
You down to the water creeping behind like old lovers
Come to watch as the moon slipped
Away into clouds and your face darkened

And I could not see your mouth
Or what your eyes might have been saying.
In the dawn I strode to the crest of the hill
And thought of you behind, sleeping still

And like a cypress or its perpendicular mind
I stood, looking down at ruins of crimson sea and rocks
And the last image of you, in disarray
And spread in your limbs; tossed to paradise across the bed.

Sarina at Santo Stefano

Not far from the old bridge
Under the celestial architecture
Of the cathedral, assembled tiers
Arches and columns of serene blue stone

Orderly artifice swooping
And rising as much as heavy
Ornamentation is able to do – launched
From a mortal creator's hand –

The wizardry of Brunelleschi
Seamed through all of this –
We wait in attendance
For you to come out

Wearing your long black lace gown
No wings attached to this angel yet –
The chorus flows round you and settles
And the baton finally falls

And voices come rising in flutes of wind
Winds as light and devilish as swallows
Spiralling higher into the surprised columns and arches…
Unexplainably lovely, I thought

Closing my eyes to the tumult swaying –
What beautiful winds do I hear?
Or is this a dream of a god, let flow
Like a gilded cloak into our muffled grey world?

Or is it just a door in heaven falling open
And the voices of angels in conversation
Floating in silvery glints to momentarily
Light up a lower world?

A vision, a sound, to see and hear in timeless seconds
And I can imagine you hours after
As I am walking through the midnight streets
Of Florence, under each pool of lamplight

You return; your body like a rag, a scarf – a veil
As you sing, wavering amongst other swaying figures
As if just about to lift and blow away in the surges of sound
Your legs and feet trailing after, head and shining hair
Following the swallows in their arching paths.

Siena

In the ebb of light
Crossing the heights above
The dull red glow of the city
Poplars smoulder apricot
As their elliptical silhouettes
Saunter up and down
The pilgrims' ridges.

The world of the hills
Green veiled in gold
Those tall trees
With feminine grace
A saintly procession
Sure of its way.
I was born by the sea
With the roar of a seashell in my ear

Light touching everything
Never too busy for love –
But now unready for this
I see dusk as tumultuous as surf
Light touching everywhere
Glowing brick, hill flanks of grass
Even the swallows threading sky
Wear the gilding as they fly

Light never too busy for love –
And then the heartbreak of dusk
Wind surfing through golden grass.

The fig

This is a time for remembering
Some of the sweetness
Slow honeyed moments
And most of them ended
Civilly, decently, politeness putting a smooth finish

To things; you felt giddy sometimes
Wondering where that rage for a cupped breast
A flexed buttock went
That hunger for nipples in flushed fingertips
For flesh happily shared and spent.
Sometimes the visions of surprise

Strike you in daylight, or nighttime
Zigzagging through like spasms of lightning – you see yourself
Like that fig tree that grew tall without warning
Now shading a stone ridge, now weathering slow dry wind
Leaden heat then whipping rain; sucking up patiently

Its store of honey; long-aged, sipped sweetness from rock.

The last lunch

Outside light glances and slides
On the Canal Grande, a varnished
Launch churns past the entrance doorway
Prow perched for seconds over curves of water.
Inside, electric candlelight glows
In discreet dimness. We sit beneath
The tall mirror, part of the slow cinema
Of a painterly setting, the burnished silver

The golden half-filled glasses, the light ripened, spinning
On rims of plates, the napkins like
A dull touch; reminders of a cheek, a kiss once…
A hush prevails. I picture us within a frame
Two gilded faces poised in time.
A work painted by an Italian master
Perhaps even Caravaggio, slowly drawing
His dividing line down two spheres of light and dark

And life – love and murder – or night and day? Shall we
Call it instead 'Dining to chiaroscuro?' Linen is
The soft texture here, your ebony dress
My crinkled jacket, a handkerchief only protection
Against the swift blooms of feeling
But love that's ending is the main question…
The loosened thread in bone-white perfection…
With remembered delicacy and grace
We pick our way through wafer-thin antipasti
The medium-rare *Principali* fillets, and finally the tingling

Citric of two matched Williams's pears. How civil is
This finishing touch to love, this calm discussion
Dissecting, slicing feelings into two moist halves.
I look up into the slanted mirror as we lift
Our entire life in gilded glasses, and true to decorum
Do not let them touch, but letting the glowing rims almost
   brush…afterwards

We sip slowly on the ruins of our affection
The Prosecco, as usual, is dry to perfection –
Our minds smile into light and dark – life's portions of once
   generous courses
Our thoughts already shifting into tidied halves
And I like to think, in retrospect, for once, my queasy panic
Stood aside to let your frowned resolve – step outside into the
   dusk light, briskly.

The Loggia, Piazza delle Signoria

Massive gods, immortals, marble mortals
On display, an aviary of murder, lust, revenge
Philosophy and rape spiralling above into space
On the granite steps stone lions prowl, guardians of chaos.

The arches merrily simulate the heavens
Leap cheekily to just below the mighty tower;
Pondering down on all this strife and deadly play –
Restrained by perfection the statues wait to come alive

Uncoiling their frozen lives; monumental patterns
Of stonework rise in ledges and then serrations
To punch a shoulder through amazed blue sky.
There is a sense of a pendulum of forces

Heaving, swishing slowly around this square
Over the milling head of the crowds – which raises
Its arms, elbows and hands and cameras
To photograph the fading galleries of history; gods staring back

Into the flashes of light, into the faces pooled upwards –
As I sip the last froth of my cappuccino
Watching a column of light sweep over
The square toward Perseus; his sword and trophy

Of a severed head – the marble bodies climbing
Up toward the arches into enraptured flight –
A woman's dowry, beauty, virginity in the balance
Patroclus limp in Menelaus's arms, shedding breaths of life –

And the cup jitters back into place, perfect in its blameless
  saucer.

The man in the Academia

It is autumn – not quite as sure of itself as winter
But gusty enough, driven on that eventual course –
The colonnades recurring like lacework over water
The canal a mirror flowing with browns

A spillway for merging yellows and greens;
In the history of sky tinged insights still alive here.
The guest writers have already packed up and gone
Taking their rumpled pages, glimpses and recollections

Back to native lands elsewhere. But there is one
Who still returns; a watcher of winters
A poet drawn to last year's watermarks
Come to note the wind's watery glints and gather those
    floating residuals…

He has booked again into memory – the same well-grooved
    room
A door in the *pensione* with bed, the desk and finally the
    window
Leaning over the canal – his mind is already inclined forward
Into the season he likes, his smile is readying to write

He puts back on the cloth of this season taking his first
    morning stroll
Glad to rediscover the colours he remembered curling down
    the canal
He takes the lesser-known alleyways to reach the old market
    place
To reread the prices of fish chiselled into maritime history

Then steps over one of the impeccable, unfamous bridge arches
Enjoying its sleeping dream, a lazing shadow below
And just twenty steps past a committee of grey
Circumspect cats – he gets to the little café where he sits beneath the faded

Stripes of the awning and relaxes, watching the tactile glide of water –
Sipping the acceptable drug of coffee and blowing his chains
Of unacceptable smoke – cordite-blue spumes into glass-transparent Venetian air.
There is no news of the other world here

There are no lists to scrunch up or to scribble here
No better or worse students, no appraisals
No nurturing of youth's febrile minds, nothing to sort out here
He sits with his own mind and his jittery companions – coffee

His conscience, his cigarettes – watching the subtle
Slower light work its glow over things; see-sawing textures
On water, the bright barbs spun on angles of bricks, the curved warm cheeks
Of terracotta – a Russian now sitting inside an American citizen
A poet awake now inside an expatriate, an exile anchored forever inside an exile
And nothing about in the sky or on the land to notice any of this, the canal flows as usual
The seabirds are circling the zone; the domes doze, doped with blueness
The gulls now quiet – are prospecting – up and down those sun-baked curves –

The browns and softer blues have it – dominating
The flow of quietness and in a gentle daze
A geared lethargy – he begins to write
The first movements – wriggles of watermarks arriving –

Lines lapping recollections – words wavering in his mind.

i.m. Joseph Brodsky

The moon, the tower and the manuscript

A salute to Giovanni Acuto – Sir John Hawkwood

The moon probes over Monte Acuto
Down through ranks of mountain pines
Strikes sparkles in the whiteness; a trace of footprints behind.

I see that window of scenery from John Hawkwood's tower
like a lingering 35-millimetre negative –
Undeveloped missive from a sketchy scene – and a porthole

Pointed into myself, my persona, shuffling under the trees; not because
I was deadly poor, then, or because this mountain in Umbrian countryside
Was not mine – my perspective was formed because I was a fugitive

From family troubles left far behind - I was a stranger, *lo straniero* –
Out of place in that light, moving like a darker dialect
Amongst the moonlit language of the trees –
Dante was there, not as my guide.

(But somewhere in history hiding.)

I remember again as Pacific waves boom diagonals
Across these memories, and
From here everything is pretty; the twinned peaks

Across the valley return just like perfect breasts, silly, yes, but
    real; true enough
As nature's nurturing company for the years I spent there in
    exile; walking
Along shepherds' paths looping round the wind blown hills –
Clambering in over fallen architraves, haphazard blocks of
    stone to explore those villages

Abandoned as much as I was then…to stand amazed in
    gaping windows.

The things I wrote were not all bad, part of myself was
Somewhere there swimming along with the long moment
Of those paragraphs, balancing a footing in an in-between
    place

Where Dante may have lived or spoken – but too young
Or over-mindful to hear or take proper note, I decided
One night and went straight to the pines and there in that
    soft glow

Of moonlight I buried my manuscript
Under the blameless snow. The earth

Was hard and cold. The spade, made and made crisp ringing
    echoes; today
I am sure it is still under there; a slab of pages tucked into
    layers of plastic
Strong enough, I imagined, to last for years like that – or
    perhaps

The plastic and pages have broken down already into useless
    traces;
A trickle left of a stranger's presence, almost a million words
In flowing cellulose, saying I am here, and lost, but not alone
    – my pen

And paper, my good friends for company – and I saw and
    described as best
I could and did not try to explain or own.
The manuscript at its best

Was the story of an ephemeral home, and then
The buried footprint of a long farewell
Scratched down hard amongst the trees…

In stark moonlight I left whatever memories
Were penned there; clear, possibly even elegant; but I did not
    come back
To find them or to write down more again – no more questions
And no more replies; all consigned to the faint enquiry of an
    Umbrian moon.

Monte Acuto, not far from Perugia, has enjoyed several fugitive
presences over time, including rebel monks; the poet Dante; and the
mercenary soldier Sir John Hawkwood, known as Giovanni Acuto,
who built towers all over Umbria.

The Naked Lunch

Her hips made a flick
A kind of signing off
A signature on spoken for property–
Then she rose to her knees
flexed on her haunches
And fell back into her muddle of limbs.

Her slow breathing fusing
A patch on my shoulder –
So I smooth her glistening hair
One finger crooked down a cheekbone
Her eyelids swoon, a flickering blue farewell
And she descends suddenly into sleep –

I think of her brown arms earlier
Filled with a snatched harvest of dark grapes
And those pink smudges among them;
Those tawny nipples jostling for space –
Her plump fruit bouncing just the same
About with those brighter reds
And ripe yellows of lemons
And an apple, escaping, rolling greenly away
As we leant together over the table –

Her giggles mimic the rippling of laughter
Before we rock to another ending
Slipping over the ledge, then sliding and
Landing like cats, on all four pads
Our tails up, our tongues pert, pink tips
Heading for the last course;
L'ultimo piatto, the final serving –
All the sweetness swirled
And consumed furiously in the next room –

Now our loose nakedness is knifed
By yellow diagonals, splashes of light
Flung down, and sideways
Through climbing Venetian slats –
And sounds of water lapping outside
Chopping rhythmically, methodically
Against the indifferent, moss-bearded walls.

The gondoliers, in their passages, cry up
To these palace windows bronzed by evening sun
Much higher than our own light-laced stone oblongs
Beyond the hired province of our four-poster bed
And the dangling remnants of a kingdom's ceiling –

The rowers cries, their rhythms, drift through two vagrant lives –
And the flesh of the lemon, its essence continues continuing
Bouncing neat yellow echoes across the ceiling
Slicing out shapes the same as our dreaming mouths.

The swallows in Saint Peters Square

The swallows refuse to assist
My eye's dismissal, tip toeing in the air
Like those minnows, suspended in a stream

Of the moment, they hover then let go
And wheeling descend to slowly rise again, no flying monk
Could pull and allow his bells to topple

Roll over so eloquently, as these unconscious ballerinas of the air.

The priests that flow in pairs from St Peters sway out across the square
And hardly lift their heads toward these tiny pendulums of flight
They grip their rosaries against the risk of an uncertain sky

And turn down the avenue in files; fluttering rags of darkness toward approaching night.

And as always I delay in this apricot-smudged square of Rome
And love to watch this autumnal show, the departure of the swallows
Signalled by their silent play, my eyes a little saddened

Want their farewell to be over quickly, my mind tucking away their salutations
But my heart tugs against this dismissal, hypnotised
By this continual swinging rhythm, a serenade to autumn

A flock of birds' last ballet in the changing rusts of light
Through a radiant gateway; time threaded for the traveller's eyes.

Tivoli

Cast as the voyeur I watch you Knidos –
And now you cannot say stop –
Here Hadrian has recreated you; your immodest curves –
Are you lovely enough, even for Sappho's swoon – I walk
 around

You, liking the way your hand does not quite reach
For the gown to cover you up; those Carrara
Nipples, your splendid triangle of pudenda; upturned eternal
 fulcrum –
Lastly the way those imagined eyes follow me;

All of your body sensing trespass; hands unsure or beguiling?
Covering or not quite covering? Is this playful theatre?
Or as natural as hesitancy? Female beauty; one shoulder
 holding fort –
Greek concepts, ancient, timeless thoughts – an Aphrodite

Conquering her Roman conqueror – as he thinks to prowl
 round her beauty;
Hadrian slanted too far over in love. Your sensual marble
Skin-tight white of loveliness; the treasured centrepiece
In a garden of an emperor's genius – and why do I find
 myself

Here? Ant slight, poised on this pavement stone of history
And how many eyes, dearest Knidos, have lusted
Or looked in abject wonder? Your fingers, toes, eroded
By weather; less of you seems so much stronger now

Suggestion completes you; you pose your exquisite
   imperfection forever –
Before the invisible emperor; his human flesh
Highness of rank, captivated by curvaceous stone –
How weak, how silly we become – male conquerors of ruined
   beauty.

And even I, not even a soldier, not to ever be immortal
With a human shrug, reluctantly turn, heart pumping
Already missing your missing eyes – missing the mock terror
   of your surprise
As I walk down the slope away from an emperor's prized
Intoxication; steps from a garden of lost glances; fervent in
   the mind.

Torte al testo

It was a lesson in cooking, or hugging
I'm not sure which, intermittent
Sizzling touches and damp kisses

Between her efforts as she rolled, lifted and pounded
the lump of dough on the table and shaped and rounded
And flattened it to fit on the flat stone

Glowing already on the fire.
An apron clinging against her perspiring nudity
She spat first on the stone's surface to see

If it was hot enough, then she lifted the stone
By its wood handle and placed it to one side
And slapped dough hard against it.

We watched the flat bread slowly browning
Our faces theatrical in the flickering light
As our lips relished more sweat and salt from our mouths

Our fingers foraging through harvests of hair
Our bellies young, quivering, tautness barely touching
Her laughter with its tiny tinkle

Broke the moment's tension before she said
Lets turn it round to the other side
'There's no egg, just salt and bicarbonate

So it will be crisper, almost like pizza.
Later she cut the toasted flat loaf
Through the centre with a long knife

And then laid strips of translucent pink prosciutto
On one half and placed the other half over
To make the Umbrian *torta* of unleavened bread

The prosciutto melting a little, odours of silky fat warm
Like touches we shared and some more
Exploratory kisses, before consuming the portions of evidence.

Umbrian moon

Golden porthole through fathoms of blue up to heaven
Soaring circular Sphinx, slowing in mid summer night air –
Sitting outside an Umbrian village bar
The withered harvester, Pino said

Gesturing crouched, with tumbler of ruby red –
God had set it all up for a game – *Un bel gioco* – and left –
Some trees he had liked to bunch together
Like sticks; rounder shapes when he played with hills;

Like we do with a trowel and cement –
After he dished up the mountains
Harvested the skies, scraped stars down
The ones he liked; others let go to drift like confetti out of
   His mind –

Here we are leaning back on this terraced ridge outside
One bulb above the door lights our world, behind
Green olives struggle to rise out of night-blue rock.
The evening seems to be waiting for Him

Moths may move but nothing much else
This July night will be still as it can immensely be
Seen and felt under stars' wheelbarrowing arcs of secrets
And the few clouds left, stopped in moonlight, after
   tumbling storms –

Only a mud coloured congress of rats leap for the corn
Hung in long plaits from the gables
A curious sort of dance back and forth
As they continue to miss one claw's hook into the lowest cobs

Or give up eventually and seep away into shadows
To scratch at whatever habit comes to a rat's mind.

Midnight heavens are perfect, tomorrow will be fine, Pino says
Downing the dregs of blood-red wine – and, he asks –
Why do these stars need us?
We look up there for Him, or for some answer

And of course it does not come –
We are not at the centre of things
We are the unfitted bits he left behind
The scattered parts of a jigsaw

He didn't explain, or try to finish – but then
When a star falls, like that slow torch there
Engraving a beautiful plume down the sky –
Wiping his mouth with a hand, the old man summarises –
I wonder always if it's a sigh still ending

Maybe a last tear of a thought; regret
In glittering sadness, which fell like a feather
Floating behind His steps
Passing from that time here, onwards.

Venetian palazzo

Dust is at rest here
It has done enough
A lacquer of finality
Borrows too much light.

Faded cherubs are voyeurs
Over an awkward four posted bed
What had they seen
Over centuries

From those arching frescoes?
Nobles cavorting, embroiled, in a storm of sheets?
That storm is long becalmed
Damask now holds down the impact

Of past loves, decades of lust, florid now silent –
Ceiling to floor mirrors
Eye sinking perspectives
Barely notice me passing

Towards a quizzical door, giving
Onto a corridor of arched windows
Cartwheeling views of the Grand Canal
Images of the sky on the move –

Time flown from greyness and paling ochres
Juggles with water and light
Shapes and reflections defiant
Frolicking with shadows from low-flying swallows.

A door slams somewhere behind
A voice trails off into the past
I descend steps from historical quiet
Back outside into a windy narrative of life.

Venice, summer ends

Water plays whimsical knave
With marble lace, freed it ripples
Like memory; arches wobble
As if doing a samba out to sea

A launch cuts through a picture
Of stone and sky, churns colours
Its wake a pulverisation of beauty
The coiling streets are ribbons to mystery

Intrigued you follow them into the ancient marrow
Of rust brick and grey stone; tight, sentinel circles
Until you reach water again; recycling
Landscapes you vaguely remember

From museums, recollections, melancholy of cathedrals –
You glimpse in the drift of the canal
A flowing depiction from a palette of squiggles;
Yellows, russets, ruby reds, crimson tears

Stretch, rippling from Titian – the art will not last
The landscape turns over like a page
Impatient to slide away downstream;
The fluted chimneys, the dozing domes

The snoozing shutters, the city sleeps
At the edge of depiction, like a noble elder
With one eye open on a wilful child
That won't stop playing with a hoop of light.

You plough toward the watching facades
Old timers lined up in the sun
Shadows withdrawn, slinking under bridges
As you speed on past; decay barely breathes the air here

But the water is still young; splashing anarchy.

Brodsky

I have not flown like
An eagle flies above your forests
I have not followed the marching Slavic conifers

With an awry nostalgic eye, I have not thrust
My wings downwards toward the glow
Of a tundra sunset dying below

The great white cliff of the world.
My precipices are more pacific
My pen slips not from cold fingers

But sweat and shudders of cicadas; humming
For an early death to life encrusted here on earth.
But yes, I have muttered down into the islands of sleep

And woken abruptly to hear the window panes
Stuttering things about floods and winds
And heard moaning from the ones still afloat in currents of the past;

In time shipwrecked, we drift, splintered masts toward the shore
Where white swans fall and crash to the sand, everywhere those curved necks shattering.
Waking I did not weep, wryly – alone in an average hotel room in Venice, as you did

As close as you could get to your family in Saint Petersburg at Christmas.
But I know like you I am one of the dreamers, in a pod of swimmers
Floating along under moonlight; my body submerged like a broken mast –

And I have walked alongside the watermarks in Venice and I have turned
Around to see the grey cats waiting for you; eyes curious only for you in midnight
Alleyways – and I have entered the room where your tears fell; glints of
Sapphires into Venice – and I suspect you did not want, from reservations –

Intense differences – to be buried beside Pound on the island of Saint Michael –
The almost neighbouring graves reached through a pathway of buried children;
So many luckless fallen angels, each with a compensating plaque –
Passing to where Olga and Ezra lie side by side

A lizard's flying leap from Iosif Brodsky; at times heartless
Precise visitor – describer par excellence – and all those
  lyrical thoughts
Now surrounded by Canaletto's water; rippling like scales of
  fishes
In tides of sunlight gliding diagonally toward and away from
  the gondoliers;

The artist's lacquered orchestra; death
With a swan's neck swaying in perpetuity.

But today, all tangled notions put aside
I take a launch to visit you both;
Each snapped mast placed several metres –
Leaps of lizards, rhymes and arguments –
Near but forever apart; under ivy, green with overflowing
  silence.

II

Elsewhere

Expatriate

Adrift, I think, is as good
A word as any
To describe this condition

After stepping from an aeroplane
To a train, then to a strange station
So many years ago, and not

Coming back, I circumnavigate
My original country, these homecoming days
Drifting in a dingy, so to speak, speaking

And dreaming in more
Than one tongue
Standing up unsteadily to see better

Where my old friends were, or
Might be still, amongst dots trickling along the shore –
The ones I knew in a life before

Whose quizzical gaze back into
My face today – defines little
More than the boy they once recalled

Who went away, vanished altogether on a certain day.
The streamers from railings to shore
Falling into the water

The thrust of the ship veering to point away
The faces framed, intersected by waving
Arms and hands, and what of that remains

That I left in a slow glide so far behind?
Enough to find a face again?
Enough to recognise a voice once more

Enough to step out of this little boat to say
Hey, hey, its me, I'm back! I'm here again!
For a recurring moment in time

I remember moving behind that boy's face
Amazed, gazing, up at an architrave
A bust of a god or an ancient gable, the light serrated

By curved edges of roman tiles, a stranger
lo straniero – in a moment of gilded silence –
Looking, absorbing, through strange, ochre-shadowed streets

Hungry always for anything more to see
Standing at beginnings and endings;
Two parts of himself, his being, his heart

Paused in the slants of a different light
The balancing of memories
Swaying together, time's pendulum
Shifting momentum, from old to newly made.

In memory of Basil

Certain light in art deco lifts
Flatters my face
The mirror and I
Repeat the journey to make sure.

Dimly in the foreground
Of the café I name Paris
(Worth a mass)
I still decline to age.

Youth clings to my complexion
Like an anxious fly
My insides refuse to rot
Perhaps red wine

Has preserved me
For one more bon mot.
Sipping the froth of a cappuccino
I remember his word agog

Balanced, surfing on foam

And dabble a bit with Bunting's
Line about cunning flies
Examining cake – (academics nibbling
On a poet's life?) Elsewhere tables

And chairs round me creak and submit

To existential meaning;
People without wings or eloquence
Who lean lovingly over chocolate éclairs –
Not cunning, just hungry

Longing for solace; reading pastry with both hands.

Postcard from Latvia

'The lost glove is happy' – Nabokov

Folding your napkin in a Latvian seaside hotel
The waiter constrained attendant, waiting for you to go
The same with the sea, a waiting wintry grey

Carelessly cresting to somewhere you do not choose to know…
In honour of the bronze thirties décor you chose
A three-piece suit to wear and a Windsor knot to eat with alone

In the huge dining room, a high-ceilinged temple to
 occasional throat-cleared silence…

The gold chandeliers glowing a garish tribute to midday…
Surprisingly the fish (a flounder) was delicious, the music
 however, a dirge of Russian
Origin, was listless as autumn leaves on the hard stones of
 socialism.

You ate your peach without knife or fork
After 'The Wasteland', no longer considered so courageous
And you thought of your youngest daughter, bored and
 married and
Pregnant, far too-soon, in snow-cocooned New York…

God how the wind here moans against those quivering hotel
 windows

Lost like the sounds of gulls dissolving in the fog
Or guard dogs or poets forgotten in Siberian prisons
Or your mind rebelling against ever fitting in…
You wonder what an old girlfriend is doing now

The one who taught you Italian in old Trastevere down across
    there in Rome?
And wore a black velvet bustier and suspenders like natural
    skin to bed
The first time you met her and who wouldn't stand for any sex
Totally naked; she described as being like having to digest
    cold toast

Unbuttered, thrown together with hotel punnets of frozen jam
And a paper serviette for luck, which you had always
    delighted in sending back
In tribute to her, especially when left to dine alone in
    grandiloquent hotels
Empty and lit as solemnly as this one, time pinned under the
    glaze of winter time…

Where the cutlery would unquietly tinkle away to itself.
Where you came avoiding distractions to try again to write
And ended up being distracted most of the time
By big-toed attempts of staff to be silent, the wry
Ongoing reflections of your several lives and lost wives
And daughters finally gone to live their lives behind windows
    elsewhere.

Rovigno; the beautiful banker

You shuffle the papers
Your fingers
Compose, recompose –
Exposing receipts
Peeled back, held there under
Your almond-shaped nails.

A girl from an echoing town
Born, raised by an ancient cantering sea –
Palaces sculpted in golden stone
Spilling their reflections below

The bulwarks of rocks in swirls and torrents
Of slowly rocking foam –
The sound of a seagull wafts
Way above these orderly rooms
Deflects our attention, and yes

I see for a second, in your eyes
Flecks of light slipping through waves
Diffused by clouds rising in measured steps
Brushing against those crumbling palaces

Images piled higher and higher in Istrian skies.
You adjust the papers, all together once more
Now done. Yes – now all can be complete.
Your fingertips press hard on a clip to confirm –

Curl and compose as before.
There on the page my name fits its box
Below like an undertow,
Your languid signature flows –

A flourish inferring now might be the time for me to go…

A brief exchange of intense goodbyes
And I walk back through the sliding doors –
Your face, your smile, bigger still
In my thoughts, while gulls, looping their cries –
Swoop and soar through the sunset's ridges of ending light.

Praying aloud

Returned – once more to the view –
Those distant mourners
Mountains of Connemara – unchanged
Beautiful and immensely morose.
The sea is smashing its pebbles, again, again
Vigour and malice churning about in waves
Gaelic an ancient language; parchments of accents in the wind.

Down in an empty church
I found you – praying aloud –
Had love gone wrong for you?
Here in the west of Ireland; her
Seesawing graveyards of stone;
Her clouds forever unfurling over

The sea and the skies' blue hope –
Your prayer pleading out to mayhem.
Today the sea's music falls crisply on freezing beaches
Groans of deeper realms surfacing in between;
Was there too much magic between us?
You vanished with an accountant

Much safer, anyway – I delayed, and then drifted away.

Sometimes in the brightening hour
You are dawn's shapely child
Emerging veiled in grey-pink gauze, and
I hear your prayers between those waves
And waves here of my own, as light lifts its veil
And a song flows over Galway, mourning that prayer that day.

A candle in the window

The single window in the room
That opens but is fixed
Is always memory.
Memory illuminates, memory
Fans a glow beyond the present
Like embers blown in a sacred fire…

Remembering between the houses
Lined along the seashore
The sea reddening in the early silence
Remembering the branches
Of the parasol pines, sweeping
Over the stars, sweeping clean the hearth

Of night, the highest tips quivering to the stars
On their arc to another dawn…
When you walked the long beach
Waiting for the ferry to take you across the water
To Tangiers; her lights little welcomes in the distance –

And how did the Sirocco blow hard, toying with your weight
Like many hands, fingers touching you everywhere at once
Then dissolving; her warmth gone in the sudden calms –
The waves oncoming, crashing into your thoughts
And the moist sand, seductive between your toes
As you looked up and saw the window in your thoughts

The window where you often sit, in another world.
And tonight, distant, it is more real than ever –
The candle you left lit, flickering over books and empty chair
Flickering over the scribbling of your absence
The far away window looking out to where you went
Bereft witness of your disappearance
Breathing welcomes, wavering meltings – always yellow.

A lull in the afternoon

for T. Kooser

The sunset fence takes
The wind-bitten trail west
Into deep white; snow sullen
Unmoved for a month, dozes

Crows cries punctuate the rises and hollows.
He disappeared before the ink
Appeared on the page, quiet as melting ice –
The unwritten final work

A poem too subtle for shortening breath to write
Doodles, letters, half written notes survive –
Now the sounds and silences can be heard
Scribbling and rustling, pauses for thoughts.

When the wind out there
Having wandered returns
With a flourish and whispers in curtains
And silence is grown, stands
In the barren room alone –
He will have returned for one last look.

Abbeville

The residence of a former Irish Taoiseach
Who seemed invincible, irreplaceable but fell from power
Like a leaf in autumn

Buildings in continual autumn;
Gloom floats, streams fragments
Leaves litter the copper-beech bordered pathway

The cobblestones are missing
A few companions, like
Teeth suddenly absent, strangely

Vanished one mist-swirled morning.
The water pump with a curving
Spout, spurts a beard of rust as dribbles

Waver from its mouth, the shadows
From branches lattice-work
The frosted lawn; a classic snap for photographers.

The stable clock has stopped turning
Dust, grit or a bird's nest has set the time to three
O'clock, if morning or during the night

We do not know; Roman
Numerals were not much use
And the time was not guaranteed to be immortal.

A piece of old plaster moulding
Has fallen past the hours
Exploded in pieces on the uncaring ground

And the small pond with its waist-deep
Neptune, is windless;
A curved swath of lilies

Set in memorial aspic.
The master is long gone now
The manor leans an inch more into allotted time.

Under the roof of a lofty winter sky
The birds forage on
Through a leafless fretwork, flitting

Back and forth, dots pausing along the blue
Glaze of ice-sleeved branches;
The scene offers not a clue
Not a hint…not one heartbeat or any rhythm

Or even a knock or scattered note of disturbance
From possible human presence, only starlings
And red-breasted robins are to be seen, snipping across the ground

Or sweeping up in clusters to a haven of cold branches.
Nothing but the life of birds moves the eye
Beyond the gaze of high empty windows

The sun-bleached door, resolutely holding its place;
The Master, inside his abandoned gilded portrait
In the naked drawing room, still impeccable

And seems, obliquely, to squint askance into time
To a spring when he rode in those high riding boots
And pleated jacket on his gleaming, thoroughbred horse

And stopped to take a cup of tea
Handed up over the prim, disciplined lawn.
The fire in the empty dining room has since flickered to a stop –

Once it crackled, happily, under a sparkling, reflecting mantle
Flames flowering in a hearth where today a few ashes
Are left, like those crushed leaves strewn about

Blown over sun-washed floorboards from an open door;

Random scatterings and other shrivelled signs
Endure, of the man departed, and his singular portrait
And his lofty myth; left to stare through a window
Down a frozen pathway, an echo of steps in a distance of time.

Achilles

He sits in silence
No armour stronger
A stone no quieter –
For a time he had lived
In sorrow, inhabited its blurred world

Hardly breathing –
Now he is again in silence
For breathing is irrelevant
After grief it goes on or does not
There comes speechlessness
And its echo; strange relief.

The art of silence
Is a stubborn art
As intricate as a spider's
Web – retelling itself, retelling
Itself; duty bound
We will have to provide

Some clumsy words for it;
But what do we know?
Sorrow keeps its own counsel
Loneliness does not share its road
Speechlessness is an unstitched cloth.
In the end we could only say

He was not dead and was here
Alive, yes – and also in heaven.

After Akhmatova

His reading after reading, as if trying
To stay alive – reading
His life of words he looked surprised
At his own language, as if it was finally escaping him

A creature coming out of his mouth
And strutting about the stage
Its persona freed, saying; not him, it's me, not him – see
I am the one who lives and speaks these things.

Then the tone lowers, on comes the decrescendo
And the voice would clamber back
Through the mouth, down the startled throat
Down deep into the lonely body again.

To shake all of its hoarded resonance
Like a fraught opera diva or better still an athlete
Flexing in, flexing out – before running
Out into the uproar, the fanfare of the stadium

Body vulnerable, breath ragged
Mind cold steel, feverish
Under the glare, roar of one surrounding breath –
Trembling to start, to run
To bring out loud unending
A cry, an end, to everything.

i.m. Joseph Brodsky

Berryman's island

Thoughts in the early morning
Can be quite powerful and form
Quickly into something musical with a rhythm

That has you walking underwater
Tugged by rip tides and bubbling vowels toward an island
Where you will surface awash with consonants through the bobbing driftwood.

Can you doff your hat at four fathoms?
The dozing fish don't have
Any expectations of an academic, or a half crazed poet

Tiptoeing over barnacles. At this hour.
You first knew your flirtation with solitude
Was already a chapter of underrated experience

To be often repeated…and while you had had offers from lovers, fairest
Collectors of endless mirrors, thimble-riggers and snide ladies who snickered
To partake a little in your silence, even to live as one together

In the goose-pimpled now; you knew solitude was not for sharing
As it was clear 'she' the muse could barely tolerate just you for company.
Solitude was deliberately hard of hearing

And would not bother to listen without a loud bang
Of silence every now and again for you to get a line through
Into the bramble of thought, past those tugging vines of conversation.

So what to do, standing back on the tickling lawn after your
   walk
Back across the underwater from the island? For the moment
You content yourself with the tingling of your bare soles and
   cold toes

In tune with the grass, sensing the stars and watching their
   quivering curves
As they slide and go by across a church spire and for instants
Solitude will brush your fingers, the muse tenderly also with
   hers.

Broken chandelier

All my eyes
Are married off
I have one pair left
Enjoying your smile

But these are older
Than a pair of torn jeans
These are lower in the water
Than a bloodshot sunset –

You are an unlikely vision
For desultory eyes; too young
For someone like me
Listening to the rain

Hammering across
The roof of his heart
The wind causing the tin to rise
And buckle high-pitched sentiments.

What has caused you
To turn back to me – trying again
To get in, here silently – inside again – you
My doll with locked open eyes

Me a sleepless ballroom
With crowding images
Too many mirrors deflecting the years –
What will I do with you my elderly child?

Orphaned again inside these doors already?
A doll propped in the gloom of my fractured palace –
Shall we dance together again down the corridor of mirrors?
Shall we glide another waltz over the glowing parquet?

Slowly moving in sympathy with those nymphs
Flying across the frescoed ceiling; turning
In time with the wobbling
Chandelier – its tears of crystal

Its years of quivering, raining down –
Round and round, around we go
As if we had fallen in love with drowning
Slower, top-heavy, off-centre, now agog

Toppling our way across a messy epoch;

Two steps forward and two steps backwards
You trying your best but you still can't cry
I manage a kind of a smile but cannot find the good-time laugh –
Dancing, dancing, coming all the way around now – aghast

Gliding feet stopped together –
Toe-to-toe and eye-to-eye –
And dread – of terrible love.

Central park and Columbus Avenue

Infinitely warm in your hand is the memory
Of her fingers entangled with yours
Wandering in the park painted with snow, windows
Like lit-up altars, floating in all four flanking views

The moonlit paths teasing your eyes into the dark into the light
Through foliage shifting ahead, beneath the rising oblongs inlaid with gold
Christmas time zipping up granite buildings into the blanketing sky.

She smiled around her turned up collar, her body
Plumply buttoned up with warmth that pulsed through
Her fingers into yours, promising more, the tepid hollow of air

Enclosed between your palms, a tryst not to be dislodged.
The snow skedaddled away from your feet
As you swung through the pinpricked tapestry of the dark

Pausing to kiss, both stroking the bark of the old sycamore tree
Where somebody, Joe, had carved a heart for Mary
The wound now healed, a ripple of growth over the scar.

You sat for a while in moonlit profiles on the bench
In unconscious harmony with the sacred tree, you were
The stranger, she was the New York native, both of you nameless

And watchful aliens, paused half way amongst the trails of trees.
You had met at Szabo's check-out counter; she with her tea, Earl Grey Twining
You with your shortbread biscuits; 'Is it time for tea?' You suggested benignly

She took you literally and by the waist; and, together arm in arm you walked
Into the streets under the stars, now both foreigners in love with the sky
In love with the golden outlines of passing strollers, their plumes of breath, no plans

To make, only the vague idea to walk contentedly together for the length of a block
Before saying goodbye in front of her building, a looming moonlit
Village in the sky. After a hug before the foyer doors, she decided in life's favour

And you ascended, smiles faintly conspiratorial in the mirror-walled lift, up past
The carpeted floors of nobody-talking-to-anyone-else floors
Except perhaps a blue-rinse lady with a manicured pink dog

Until with a click and a buffeted shudder you were walking
Inside, across her abundant metres of parquet-patterned floor.

The park was a better backdrop to be with a mysterious
    stranger
She had said, pulling me out onto the terrace
Where we hugged, cosy in our wonderful warm strangeness
Under the same moon that patiently waited, had glazed the
    park to gold for us.

In the morning buoyed by bouts of love and tenderness
You slipped on your jeans and shirt to go down for milk and
    coffee
After shopping you returned to the foyer

A harvest of things in both hands as you walked into the lift
    then soundlessly
Ascending you remembered you had forgotten to remember
Her door number and her floor and her name you had never
    asked for.

Fear of life?

I've lost my fear of death
It's somewhere down there
Underneath the clutch or brake pedal

I don't dare reach a hand down and get it
Or I might cause a bad accident…
Like the squiggle-shaped girl

Waiting for the lights to change.
A voluptuous corkscrew locked in her curves; a fancy
Accident in her own right.

If I was in a good place
And mood, and she designed the time…
Who knows what kind of loops

Overpasses, spaghetti junctions we could invent
And then circumnavigate?
Today I cruise the whole way through

Up and down and round and around the roundabouts, fearless

Instinctive, peerless in all swift slipping gears, fit, ready for anything
I glide through the memory of my rusted errors
Chance is a smiling blur along the side my shining shape

Fear is now down there, somewhere between the banana skins
The lottery tickets and the flattened accelerator;
Subdued – squashed in the clutter under my tapping, grooving feet.

Five seasons at Portlick (all in one day)

Before the lake of the Celtic kings –
Lough Ree – four seasons race across a sloping field
Scampering winds, tiptoeing flurries, scattering rain, suddenly clearing…
Darker light chasing sunlight into the waves of beeches
Copper leaves sweeping and swaying
Sparkling with swaths of sequins
Or silver flares squirrel upward into fleeting light…

Until the clouds slow and cease to move
A long breath out of time, light darkens now
And they have stopped; a lilac range rises above
A Brazilian sunset, spreading
Out to inflame the sky; climbs in orange
And crimson and mauve ridges –
Riders in torn overcoats canter across
The top of the highest, until they spin and turn
Tumbling around, wheeling away in wisps

Like ragged remains of fleeting thought…
The bellowing conifers, now dead quiet
Are standing in their breathless plumage
And limp skirts of leaves deepening into mauve and crimson.
I am the fifth season, an unturned page, unknown seeker of seasons here
Distant summers roll southward in white waves behind my shoulders…
Today I stand and watch as the stranger here, at home with another strangeness
Before a blowing, white-capped Lough Ree day…

Standing evergreen, watching the flourishes
The scattering steps of a whimsical, whirling, blind fiddler's Ireland.

Gull Man

The unending lament
Of the gulls, airborne choruses
Hovering or spiralling
Down winged wells of light –
Where have I not heard the gulls?
Slants of sound, plumbing the sky
Everywhere on the wild shores of this country?

Are they souls – souls of mothers?
Souls of wandering, luckless children?
Souls of lovers long lost –
Souls of the gone; blank gaps in time?
Or simply gulls, creatures of flight
Of splintering brightness, just there
Metres above the rounding roar of the waves?

Perhaps they really want to tell me something
As I walk along the bluish curve of an untrodden beach –
Watching how they sway in dots above the cliffs
As I follow intrigued at how they glide
Just above the spray – back and forth
Over and across the crests of undulating waves.

The long-haired gods are here this dawn, rising in lace
Gathering into a merging mane, diving down
Into greener, preferred underworlds.
Now, as I pause, ankle deep in streaming water
I think I know what the gulls are saying
Or singing in their bittersweet way.

Suddenly, in those bobbing choruses, as they
Hover; swaying artfully in air, I hear them cry:

Yes you, yes you below, you are just humans
And we up here are only just birds – pity,
Such a pity – we were never created
To fly, to dive and fall and rise, as one creature!

Heaney's wind

Stopped by the cliff edge
Standing close by the rocking car –
Torrents of wind flowing and you catch
Still holding the freezing door handle –
A sudden blow of comfort…

You are reminded of Heaney
His slow stoic lines of verse
Driving those four muddy wheels further
Hunched in his cosy car island
Slowly following the cliff's edge in County Clare.

His thoughts bucketing sideways
His heart buffeted suddenly upward
Like a kite twisting and turning in the sky –
And you stand away from the shaking vehicle
Freed of the cold, chrome grip

Watching the glow of a sunset, a galleon in flames sinking
Your thoughts tugged closer to the cliff…

Standing away from the shuddering province of your car
Facing the light's rush, while it floods into every crevice –
Even your saddest secrets…sluggish in the leaps of light
And you suddenly grab for your hat, flown

Into the streams of light and emotion…
A favourite old cap, gone with a gasp
Wrenched from somewhere in your guts, your wings
Of curses floating up too fast –
Flying beyond your stretched, transparent hands.

Ikos then

Swallows of light
Above the sea
Windowsills shallow again
The sea woken, surprised
In her rumpled blue nightdress

Her night-long panther roar
Spilling, fading into early light
Wavelets causing pebbles to lift
And click in delight, one gull, messenger
Glides past, then another, the sea has

Settled, readied itself for the sun
Merciless, universal, to come and stare noon
Down into its parted depths –
A harvest of light continues
The sea glimmers, shifting intense blues

Now painterly-like, waits; an absorbing paleness
Ready to share the sun's golden brush
To dip and flourish, glittering edges to the horizon.
My body, weakened again by flooding light
This air delicious, an onslaught of sensual warmth – decides, time

To get up – limbs flexing the prospect of a walk
Into the framework of this depicted day after day –
Life here, languidly lived, is often too good to be true –
I shall set off with sandals and battered straw hat
Trousers I slept in, cuffs rolled unevenly up

Shirt half unbuttoned, I may not wear the hat; allowing
Some sky-golden madness into my head
Waving it feebly to fend off curious gulls
And the seas murmuring insistence –
Not quite the midday Englishman

I shall come blundering, still fumbling with sleep
Into the sun-bleached, wind-painted village
Nose following the odours of fresh-baked, crusty bread
Sniffing the hooked arabesques of dark coffee –
Tomatoes and garlic are on my mind

Basil and mozzarella and virgin olive oil next to buy
I shall loll under an awning talking dreadful Greek
Saturated with the veil of the morning
Sipping caffè latte and eating almond cake
With the dimmer light of some verse
Half written on the back of the receipt –

My proverbial dog lost already, hunting madness into a brighter haze.

Ikos

The room on the other shore
Of the island, every window
Broken, was your borrowed home
For months of that unchanging summer.

You watched it glow to life
Every morning, during the day
Its lazing moods playing around the walls
With varying skies, until the long golden tide

Of the eternal evening; that time
Seems like the life of someone
You were still getting to know
Someone lean, agile, someone who lived for the sun

And loved a beautiful girl. The bed was narrow
An anxious fretful thing, but it did not matter
You slept rapt, entangled through time –
Mornings swimming in the early light

Four legs dangling, torso and breasts
Bobbing, undulating together
Translucent water swinging you both
In its rocking Aegean – ancient wet warmth.

Rocks crouched to watch you;
Dark brothers at night, sleek blue sisters
At dawn; shoulders touching; with a blurring wind
To dry you, eternity spoke the wide sky

Silver emigrations spoke the midnight sea
The moon wrote golden testaments
Across upturned faces; all that in ruins
On the day of the leaves, streaming this way, that way

Like frightened mice; limbs of trees refusing everything
The sea leaping around you like so many dancing goblins
The sadness of the little boat, struggling forward
Toward another coast; another land obsessed with its own light;

Its wild charges of darkness, its rain wired
To foreshores blurred to greyness; summer
Torn into rags, tumbling behind, surfing in curves
Back toward the sisters, crouching, mourning

Now transforming to cloaked brothers; misfortune
Forgetting to close the broken windows, and
In the rocking, tormented boat
The resentful seething of the wind;

Memory still unforgiving in your fingers
Flexed, rubbed after the vanished smoke of a match.

Lost realms

Once they tried to break the studded door down –
History always ready to repeat itself
Crashes again, back into good old basics – like rape and pillage.
All, however, is quiet today. Wives hiding in the tower
Are only parts of a quill's dried memory now.

Clocks inlaid in walls and over doors
Have long done enough; time moves in silence
On flecks of lint – a palace living inside walls of memory
Only light burning through leadlight windows
Slants here and there; muffled steps cross, recross

Polished boards; your young still remembered face
Looks up from pools of sunlight here and there, now there is so little
Furniture left; Baroque and Edwardian swept into dimmer corners
The curtains gathered at the waist and hip
Are like old courtesans, curvaceous yes, but limp

Swaying empty of breath…on one mantelpiece
A small portrait left of a daughter who floated
Off into the shining of an awful future, behind a door
A shadow of a wife, life size, inanimate –
A victim of a husband's long and cunning knife –

You pass under chandeliers spared removal
They elegantly regret the glow of the fireplace below –
Crystal tears sometimes flicker hints of flames
If your glance is quick enough; you wonder
If a pet monkey that saved a baby Lord from engulfing fire

Still haunts the burnt-out attic – outside the facade
Was famous – glazed onto biscuit tins, holly and chocolates
Ye olden castle decked with bells – it kept centennial Lords in Port
And Stilton – until a damned copyright expired – from the galleried kitchen
Its din of pans and hiss of vapours; tunnels go all the way from iron stove to

Grove – where picnics in regalia were held; silver and crystal
Arranged under the shadows of ancestral oaks.
You cross the room again, trying not to remember
The diamond ring your great-aunt dangled on her finger
At the engagement lunch – her ample breasts
They wrote; a lovely pronouncement
Set amongst the ruffles – you, young dreamer, touched her painted cheek

With mistaken notions of belonging – but that is enough of nostalgia now
The curtains will suffice to remind you of her devastating hips
And anyway memory is only welcome here
In gradual doses, like a good guest you need to check
Eventually with Dun and Bradstreet – the hall mirrors

Are best left empty – a smile from a century behind your
    shoulder
Might strangle you – outside the vaporous view was always
    perfect
Where once a garden would cure itself in timeless order –
Now irreverent pelting rain is drenching overgrowth
The hedges running away like green-cloaked rogues

The roses entangled in their own feet
Tripping amongst vulgar, lurid weeds –
Petals bloated and sickly
Swinging loose in the torpid breeze –

Again thrilled by echoing steps
You enjoy the hall's indifference
Its recent disdain for introductions, its welcome
Now a habitual, smudged praise – along the barren walls
You remember your great-uncle's portrait and as you turn the
    corner

Where you first heard the glasses tinkling
And imagined the fire's roar, now you find a singular absence
A hovering silence – all the lords and ladies (and hidden
    mistresses) fled –
You are the last to count their imagined shapes
Like ghosts unshackled from grey, hunchbacked regrets...

But here on the floor is a round miniature
Framing an unusual view of an eye
Is it the talisman of a tormented soul?
Or is it some plaything, a charm – a spell-caster
Dropped from an ancient, sinister dimension? –

The eyebrow is a curled moustache
The puffy eyelids are two lips
The eye itself opens like a mouth
The eyeball a shrunken tongue, the pupil
Is the tip of a mind's thought; squinting from a ruined palate?

You will take this home with you, quietly back –
Back through the servants' buried tunnel, through the
    Garden Grove
Where you brush away a tear, a smear of her quivering breasts
Down the crunching drive and through the iron gates
Until the public road, the circling ravens, the storm-wrecked
    trees

Where you can walk, safely forgotten
Alongside grinding traffic, humdrum of the present moment –
With this strange little quizzical porthole –
This timeless world's eye; a souvenir
Of forgotten realms – staring its silence inside your pocket.

Orderly encumbrances

Simple but ingenious;
Drawers; shelves of displaced time
Strayed dust; dehydrated blood –
The cat and the little girl
In the photo of my wedding
Sharing red bulb eyes.

From top to bottom drawer
In a desk of rolling relics
Twitching reminders
Grimaces hooked or snagged –
Could be from too many divorces
Anything rising to the surface

Saved from each Titanic; something the child
Grabbed to stay afloat; silver buttons
With crowns and anchors, pennies
Green with resentment – foreign currency
From a tribe of uncles – a smug lover
Who gave me a manual on anger management?
And belted me over the eye with the hard cover.

After the Cub Scout badge (where are they
All now?) And before I close every drawer;
A yellow wildflower dried between pages
Of mother's unfinished book: *Bleak House*.
A fly adjudicates my fruitcake –
It's good at this, but still academic, still not quite sure.

Tea gone cold, from thinking left on.
I should go out, but where? Friends
Mercilessly dead; unseen drifting relics –
Silence, sliding back and forth
In the drawers of memory –
Shakes dust and lovers back to life.

Portlick Castle

built by Hugh de Lacy, in 1192

Beautiful but forgotten in the modern world
She stands guard, battlements and tower
Stalwart forever against the Viking invader
Ghosts of invasions sailing across the Irish lake
Lough Ree; the Norman place of the great stones

And chaos of clashing axe-wielding armies, battle cries of
    Celtic chieftains;
It is rumoured a noble Celtic prisoner strides through
The bowels of the cold stone tower, and when he does
The din is incredible, chilling the mind of the recent visitor

As he clanks, long-haired, dragging his sword across the
    echoing room.
The landscape here is benign, layers of time and rich sodden
    earth
Cover old blood, savagery and many conquerors' sardonic
    amusement –
Sown over and over again, furrowed under for as long as the
    oldest folk

In the village remember; the pasture ferments to a slow
    moving sunlight
And the fields grow sleeker greens under a gentle spring sun –
Church spires of the abandoned Anglican faith
Glisten in the day's cloud-spilt light, or sail gleaming through
    the fog and rain.

Some days the wind plays games sending on its little hawk
   nosed
Waves, swiftly with no warning from the depths of the lake –
Where it is said the ancient king still sits, enthroned always
Amongst the murky currents, eating his snatched pike

With two brine-pickled hands. And the light
Sweeping across the lake, rising over the slopes
Hits the tower every so often, deflected and dulled by a
   churning cloud
And the flash resounds against the tiers of stone

Like light from silver cymbals; and the statues of poets
And marble fairies, shudder alive for seconds in the garden
   and the great urns murmur
Like groans resonant from a giant's mouth and the
   percussions of light
Travel the orderly lawns and pass through the high conifers
   like ghosts

Into the fields beyond; where cattle barely notice, grazing the
   slopes
Back and forth from the shore of the lake; now serene and
   waveless.
And I remember the years of different light I lived there
   reminiscing secrets
While ghosts of an older Ireland
Enjoyed the dank rooms
A step or two, a door or two, ahead of me.

Return to the west

'Ah, lover by unwearied lover' – W.B. Yeats

Yes, it would be good
To drive the same road
Into the descending sun
Again to reach the coastline
The blues of sea and sky

Good again in the slow redness
To watch a great white swan turning
As the glittering water faded
To walk the estuaries and shores
Of Galway – to turn and look

At the grey light and mist over Connemara
And hear once more the sea, crashing
Its welcome, welcoming with the gulls' penitence above
Good for sure to go to the place
Where the girl prayed aloud

Her fervent whispers in an empty church
Answered by their echoes. Today
I received mail from someone
I had not seen for years, who passing by my place
Thought to visit and remember.

Rereading words I remember
How stone towers there dripped in November
How April mist hung in oaks, like conspiracy
How rags of light swept overhead in the winds
And the doors hanging awry, echoing my first steps inside
The banging applause right through the place

As the draught swung lockless doors shut and open shut
The building waiting for its owner
The rooms listening to years of silence.
Yes it would be good to ask that kneeling girl to rise
And hand in hand to walk from the cool
Into sunshine, and standing there, eyes blinded
By the light, decide against what really happened.

But all this shall have to be something
Revised in memory, for she is long gone now.
And although the swans return always
And turn and turn and turn
And the mist and rain waving its cloth
Blows and flutters over Connemara – and the sea still waits

Swirling words and thoughts I did not say
I did not say – and I still hear her prayers
And see her kneeling there
While in the arch of sunlight
The gulls sweep and rise and cry
Kneeling while the waves keep on falling
And here far away her whispers
Fill my heart, like the waves rolling
And rolling, filling the bay of Galway
Waves crashing out solitude – crashing solitude and welcome
Waves roaring and whispering
Solitude and welcome
Crashing out endings, beginnings of prayer.

Remember Anektoria

'The early Christian church wherever it could, burnt the writings of Sappho' – unknown scribe

Sappho ended the myths
The celestial battles
Her voice yearning for
A remembered lover's face
Kisses lost, promises in those glistening eyes.

An image swirled with aloneness into lyric.
Loneliness pulling stronger than chariots
Stronger than gods and goddesses colliding in historical skies;
Marble cracking at the ankles in flight
Sudden fragmentation – and porphyry hurtles into dissolution.

The loved one had gone from her
Her loneliness followed, orbiting in loose lyrics
As she sleeplessly turned, searching, remembering
Like a long beam sweeps its way across oceans of darkness.

Loneliness darned her words
Into a lacework of grief;
Embroidery of yearnings
Whisperings threaded into circles
Widening patterns – to reach her lover's eyes.

Rilke's Torso

Out of the torso, all we appear to have left
Of courage, grace and power
Is a surfacing question…

How much grace
How much strength, could remain
Braced against such wreckage?

Under the skylight the torso blazes
Before our eyes, its straining legs, the fire left
In its belly – its contemplating, time ravaged head

Are the dispensed extras, absences
Hovering in the air, an audience
Of vagrant question marks

Waiting above our darting minds.

We stare at the glowing shoulders, trying
To reform all the missing bits
But the torso, alone, survives

Our meddlesome enquiry; and limbless
Headless and eyeless
It flexes shining pectorals

And speaks from its ellipsis
And seeks from its sightlessness
With a peculiar light outstaring our eyes.

Syros

We walked to the shore
Man and woman; islands
Holding hands, our blue eyes caverns
That knew each other

Our feet together
Conversing in frothy toes.
The sea was kind, speaking in languid
Skipping tones, throwing down

Its tinsel, tinsels of tones.
You picked up a shell
And pressed it into my hand
I held it to my ear; resonance

Whispered inward, like a long hoarse kiss

I licked some Grecian salt from your lips
Fingertips uncovering ancient kelp
Tangled in your thoughts and hair; the murmuring water
Rocking the empty sky; our bodies undulating realms;

A trembling pair of terracotta heads; shoulders, waists, legs
Like famished flames lengthening, heading bravely out to sea.

The Bog at Clonmacnoise

It was a long time ago I was standing
Here, on a soft day, rain ingraining
The green weave of fields, the enormous
Stone crosses shedding drops of greyness
Shouldered by Ireland's preoccupied heavens.

Today the fields of rye
Are brightened by sunlight that skims
Over summer-ripe blades of grass
And cows graze slowly through islands
Of yellow and purple wildflowers, where Vikings
Rose in roars from bumping prows of curved ships
To murder, rape and spurt virulence into another village.

Liscannagh stone is strewn in dark worm-eaten surfaces
About old sacred grounds, where the gravestones slope
   forward
And back; swaying toward the west like dazed pilgrims.
   Thumbprints
Of grey, black and orange lichen smudge

Across names of the now forgotten dead –
The Shannon River swings a languorous hip
Through the bustling bulrushes, the bog's
Carpet of chocolate brown flows under slow brush strokes
Of light; yellow columns pour from oceans of rolling cloud

While women bog-cutters harvest the speckled peat around
Nimble feet, clicking blades unearthing glints over the
   estuarial-like surface –
Some bright and bare-legged girls, caught by the eery light
Manage to harvest some of the sun in orange and pink
   bikinis –
A moment to get limbs browned under the midlands'
   brooding air.

The wind begins to drub up through
The runnels of roofless stone churches, warbling
Up through artfully bricked slits of sky –
The gothic arches are like palms

And curved fingertips, pointing to heaven
In ragged prayer, the slabs of stone
With tides of inscribed names, seem to roll
Recklessly, down the long grassed slopes to the river

Darkening in the dusk – now the bog-harvesters
Have all vanished; slipped away with the shadows
While surges of wind begin to cluster in arches and entrance-
   ways
Of disembowelled churches, moaning, whispering along the
   ragged ridges

Capped with patrols of seagulls, turning around, stragglers
Still left in the twilight, before they finally rise and strive
    higher
Flying onward again, white and grey emigrants, drifting in
    glints, in long shining
Sweeps toward eastern Galway and fading at last into the
    hovering flames of the west.

---

* Clonmacnoise was founded as a religious settlement on the Shannon river, between Lough Ree and Lough Derg, in AD700, by Saint Kevin.

The Dead Poet

Once a Swedish poet
i.m. Harry Martinson 1904–78

If you step outside the cabin door into the chill of the morning
And you look about where you knew he went on his walk –
And following the trail of a moose or the paired pricks of a
    hawk or raven
You might still see a footprint of his, surviving the days
    already gone...
And then go to the mantled cairn of stones on the crest
    where he paused in summer
To watch the white birds swing and glide over the furrows of
    ploughed land
As he stood knee-deep in grass blown furious by the wind
His cap in his hand and his hair threading the flow of air.

However it is probable you will not find him at first
Even if you peer further into the half-dark forest...
You may turn in a circle with your eyes upturned to the sky
And also be no wiser, but if you crouch and keep silent he
    might return to you
In a sigh of wind or in a leaf that may tumble onto your
    shoulders or your head –
For the poet is just as present as the cool air now hovering
    over blue ice and snow
And look and you will see how some of him falls in the dry
    white powder
Drifting from the wind-ruffled branches of conifers as they
    swing and sway –

And to the west on a clearer day some of him drifts high above
The depthless blue aura of the mountains
And down here nearer, a part of him will always be there
 hovering
Over the landscape of marching forests
And floating like a page blown every way
Over dips and rises of the sun-yellowed plains –
And his words, spilling, now streaming closer, are shadowing
 pure white ground
Like the seeker birds swooping over the rose-tinged snowdrifts.

Dust and time

You stare into boredom
Like an art form
A window
On monotony.

This is not like gazing at lint
Or dust descending
In a space of minutes
In air made golden –
That is focus.

This is becoming utterly
Insignificant, watching nothing much
Happen – it is as if the dust
Actually watched you – the lint
Descended to get a better
Look at your paralysis.

These tiny specks
Will continue to descend
After the human they examined
Is spent and buried – after you are cleared
From the shelf;

'Remember me,' you whisper
But the dust does not listen.

No door to a stone

There's no way in
So leave me alone
Says the stone's absence
Of expression – no use looking
For the cleft – I like myself as
Intractable, it took a hundred years
Of caressing currents
To become as smooth and as inscrutable

As an egg; a good stone
Does not share a chink of its intentions
I thought you knew all this – best to give up
Trying to fathom me – so throw me far away
With all my secrets; skimming across waves
Or arching far over through the air. I don't care
Timeless secrets are weightless
I'll fall with them into deeper, darker water

Or into tangled native grass;
Waiting under the drift of sand grains
Long grass or snaking seaweed, giving
Nothing away, listening
To the ancient, humming silences
Sealed tight against light, sky and time.

The waves tell them

You put the book of Greek poetry down
The lines, like tiers of streets
That led down to the blue wall of the sea

Watched from pages inside – have led you to here as well. Words
Written like those know how to tiptoe
Into the softest part of your heart and know

Well how to resonate also with words
Of the world you have read elsewhere, the streets
You have seen, the words you have even said
Elsewhere, all of these are echoing here.

Resonance chimes to the length of time it has taken
To arrive, here the remembered beach is not quite the same –
The woods on the headland are very close but just not the same

To what you have known, but they say the same things. They say solitude.
They say some of this beauty will be yours, gifted, if you look enough.
They say the miracles of light; the cloud-streaked cycles of the sky

Are there as an offering, you should learn to accept and take.
You have seen how the aged sit with their backs to the reddening sea
The waves falling behind them tell them what they have known already

They watch a cooler sky, turning eastward – the night coming again
Descending with its unravelling cloak of stars, while
The bloodbath of sunset; its holocaust sinks behind them into silence.

For two seasons here, you have walked the highest
Street above the ridge-perched town, along the last uneven edges
The headland of parasol pines; trees now the tall children

Of the seeds of roman trees, carried by their searching galleys
And zigzagging trade and foraging northern winds. The rocks here have
Tumbled long ago into places time gave to them, the high trees

Of umbrella-like boughs which time has taught to swing and creak; wheezing their song
Into this midnight wind; below grottos yawn down into darker mouths –
The icons of Saints, Mermaids and Madonnas bob above rocking blues and greens

Left for limp, unlucky fishermen – or pregnant women swimming inside for a blessing
And storms always content to disturb, lurching the waters about their echoing wombs.
And what have I learnt, thinking and walking, down these streets

Of squat, limed houses – whiter under a full moon than ever in sunlight?
Perhaps only that in this moment, it feels right for me to finally leave.
The days of seductive peach and yellow endings, can now no longer beguile me

Like they did once, or my lazing, wandering mind into any further delaying.
The ridges of molten, melting skies, the biblical clouds, the winds streaked traces
Have now a weakening power to persuade; the stars still have their way

To gleam within their curved clusters and herd the swings of tides away
But I am only a minuscule part, an unlit filament, a flicker in all this.
A kind of seed that has not begun yet to learn to learn the whisper for falling in flight –

And I no longer want to curb, to deny my need for new uncertainty
And smother my desire for what the road may wind ahead to meet
Where these swarms of stars and nights of tideless beauty
Cannot calm time, change dawns, dusks or nights
Or hide my heart's growing infidelity.

Syros and the last sunset

It is the last day on this island
Where you have dived
Through the schools of currents
To reach the sea anemones clustered
On the clear bottoms – sandy troughs
For passing fish and loping octopus

And walked up and down the dusty tracks
Over crests and down to other bays and inlets
And learnt to love the turgid tongue of yoghurt
Learnt to toast the evening sky
Through a raised globe, a prism of green wine
And eaten the rustic cooking with a faux shepherd's relish.

Walked to the crimson shore
And let the evening sea of redness reach your toes
As you sip on the wine's pert bitterness
The salt in everything now – brine in your wave slapped
 thoughts.
The wind has dropped; the sea is a taut burgundy skin
Silence speaks its own soliloquies

Thoughts of missing all your new-made friends
Swirl through your closer inspections
Of miniature marine residents, left to shift
In rock pools until the dawn brings its bouncing, gushing tide.
The light comes forward, towards you on its last retreat
From the collapsed wreckage of the sun, but this is not the end
The last serenade to one remaining day, only it's repeated

Ritual, where we, like curved receptacles, remembering what
    light
Does – watch it and then fill up inside slowly with it –
    constructing more memory
In the perched opening of our mind, my glass, my mind and I
A cup, a chalice and a window
Held open to blue air floating above – with the distant
Specks of birds scattering into cries toward the west burning

And the golden haze moving as an endless ending
Never and forever to be remembered in my flickering brain –
Light seeping toward the uncertain edges of a sky and further
    darkness
And neither will the Mediterranean trees cease clinging
To reach and sleeve these rags of golden light –
Images congealed once day has flown into the clefts of the hills

And the wind-folded grass and the stubble higher up
Racing upward so fast, slows to fade to greyness, and the sky
    waits
In arched silence – witness to what was made and unmade
Set around us here below – and I know the straggling she-
    oaks left, and myself
Will be the surviving witnesses to all these whispered soliloquies
Retold to myself as I make my way, sailing tomorrow, moving
    away
Across the sea – in the days of light to stretch for miles into
    the blue ahead.

III

Love and other trouble

Nardia

Without a calling for poverty
You learnt its crust
Young on the road
You tore at its marrow;

A sponge for wine, broth
And clarity, clearness
That forgave youth's electric clutter
Light that shone in things.

With little money, sparseness
Made beauty stark
Grace, naked a natural art
Eventually she was there

At the table in front of you
You knew little enough
But you sensed her beauty
Was a surprise, an unplanned gift?

Either that or divine intervention –
Years after, in streets of dreams
You still toss her kisses
Like pennies, flipping

Through the light and wind.

Aphrodite?

So you leapt at last
Head out of a cresting wave
Light on your back
Like a dolphin
Curving down

Vanishing into the foam.
It was as if a veil had
Been drawn back
And cast away and from
A different light

I looked into your
World of raining light
Moments pouring when you
Flickered from girl to fish
Fish to girl, and later

When I remembered
You walking out from the sea, fingertips dripping
Hips glistening sparkles of light;
The roars shaking in droplets of water
Your kiss – a mix of grit, saliva and hisses.

Swallows inside

Even though the sliced
Parma ham is silky
Even though the Umbrian wine
Is Rubesco and smells temptingly
Of berries, plum and furrowed *chernozem* –

The fig delicious – your lips are tired
You sense a wan swallow inside you
A creature circling a room of your mind
Colliding again with glass – what will startle
Your senses to come alive again?

Turn the wheel of your thoughts
And sail over a cliff?
Fall roaring out of being?
She stands in the light of the doorway
Body pearly in weightless cotton

Nipples, disturbing smudges
A thigh classically provocative –
(Who do you think you are – 'Venus
Of the View', by chance?)
You are teasing your nipples

Like old wounds, scabs – plucking them

Like a game to see who swoops first?
The dark swallow stirs
Flutters from your darkness, glides
Toward the sparkle in her eyes –
You lift your fork; loving the filmy fat – perfect with the lean.

A bumpkin heart

You said, I offer love –
I say for what?
Something in a perfumed envelope –
Pressed down, waxed and sealed for who's freedom?

And so will we hammer
And fashion curvature, then wear
The same, inseparable breastplates?
And fall in battle together, godlike

And beautiful together, your hair
Shining, swathed across my bronze chest?
When they cart the wounded and dead away
They will see where a chink in our armour

Defeated us – where a well arrowed cliché hit home and
    crippled us –

Or a lie more ruthless than truth
When a rusted, trusty blade
Was plunged into our backs, through
To each heart, chilling life up to its hilt.

Love is to start with – another untended wound.
Amongst the scars of a past where
History always tried to repeat itself
Whether we ran or hid or did not know how to hide.

Your noble fingerprints
Will not be found, covering
The others trespassing over my heart
All traces removed, erased in that unforeseen swoon

That felled us together with an echoing blow
In the spring of the beginning of hope.
My bumpkin heart is my Achilles heel
If I survive your love

I will suffer much more
Than just betrayal –
I will suffer another
Burdensome survival, unless I become

By strange decree – or fabulous chance –
A demigod – and then cease to be
And forget any need to feel, and soon enough
Depart to search for those untenanted pedestals –

The Belvedere's of the frozen heart; oh!
Such silence in those abandoned gardens –
The shadows in the ivy, my new lovers
Creeping through a tide of leafy

Green-gold moonlight; climbing statuary;
Painstaking patterns reaching over plaster
Stretching higher to the last crack widening in my breast
And the wound zigzagging inside –

Where my heart is forced asleep
In memory, forgetting how it was to bleed.

And love of hide and seek

And love comes from your mouth
Breathless pleasure confessed in air –
And thoughts returned in dazed words
Become touchable in shuddering breath, something

Blown, a verbal pulse, desires slurred
Love as air scarcely heard, expelled
With its measure of foibles, bubbles
Magical tints of terror – whispers of comfort.

Under blazing vine leaves love invites
And warms, floating in the air
Like murmurings of sunlight
Like humming somewhere of meticulous bees

A swarm approaching, flowing past an arc of fountain water –
Leaning daydreaming trees; the sway of golden leaves
Kisses sealed, moist beneath pendulums
Of lazy light and shadow, and

In your secret, tinkling place
A space amongst the sheltering leaves
You both lie embraced, half awake, half asleep
While the whole world looks, and thinks it sees.

Apricots and cumquats

For days I watched you walking
Through the marketplace
Gulls cries above and wings gliding around you –
How those naked sandals on your feet, amazed

And hair unkempt but carefully tumbling so
It tossed articulation when you spoke –
And then you reached and picked up fruit; an apricot
Always was your first choice, and your preferred theme it
  seemed –

A skimpy orange dress
Suntanned legs unhindered by the floating cotton –
In autumnal slants of sunshine
Your hair curling with its light, flecks as free as floating leaves

Unfolding reds and russets against the walls of tidal green swells
Breeze-blown threads across the travertine pier –
You were tall amongst the older women's scarfed heads
Through the sun-bleached green umbrellas…

The recurrence of the sea's echoes heaving against travertine
Seemed an undercurrent to your course
Through stalls and barrows in the windy square
Giddy green water looming, crashing against your conversations

Made often through cupped hands…
Soon I learnt to follow, a little careful
Not to get too close, buying apricots and cumquats
And then for good measure, oranges and mandarins;
  appearing to be

Circling there for no other reason – innocent or complicit
Furtive or urbane – ridiculously I strayed along behind you –
Until several days later when the sky had changed
Displayed in colder streaks of greys and yellows

And you did not come again
And I had the market
To myself for three or four or more days –
And then for weeks afterwards…

My bowls and oval plates
Placed on the window ledges –
Became still lives – depicting to a wintry square
Your absence, arranged in mandarins, cumquats

Oranges… And the tawny silence of apricots.

Injuries

In the mirror
I have two arms
And one more, missing.
The one that clasped
Your shoulder close
The one that helped
So I could kiss you.

Things go missing, life like
An addict to theft, pilfers things
Absences fill space – may survive
Like laughter, years later –
The kiss returned still warm
On the floor, trodden on
Like fallen petals

Is not good enough. I
Do not stoop
To pick up nothing – I
Stand still, erect, shoulders
Squared and look at myself
And imagine she is there again.
The mirror does not lie

It says she is not there –
Nothing you can say will make it lie –
Was she ever there?
Yes, she was, there beside you
And there's still proof, see
The left eye of yours is missing – the one
That saw her last, before leaving.

Love not the wind

Is the culprit – the wind rolled past for sure
Swept through our roaring minds
Rattled over the terrified roof
The wind drove light deeper or right away

From stone, grass, leaf, wild trees
Then swirled and went out again;
A flock of pages taken for a dress –
Diva feigning her pure simplicity.

She blew hillsides into ragged fringes
Flailed grass along the thin path we walked
The wind knew we were in awe of it
And blew our hair backwards, what a laugh!

But love was so very subtle
It did not blow or bluster
It did not speak
It slinked in insinuations
And slowly stole all our truths.

Lunch in Napoli

We bounce around the city
In your mouse-sized fiat
Buildings jostle above our roof window

As you drive like a minnow
Weaving through shoals of bigger fish.
We swish under the castle and we glimpse Vesuvius

Watching us as we lurch
And straighten from a circle of staccato blurs
Neapolitans, captains of equestrian traffic swerving…

The woman singing on the radio
Has a voice you could squeeze like fruit
With its clotted lisps of mystery; a soft interrogative
    continuing…

Mouse parked, we grab our tickets and hustle through the
    aquarium
Hungry, in a hurry, we pass from fish dozing
Stacked from top to bottom in tanks, to the *trattoria*, to the
    view of the sea

From the terrace like a rolling cloth of flecked green crests
We start to eat the cousins of our placid friends inside
Fritto Misto – nice, crisp outside, crustacean and fish heaped
    together

Prawn and whitebait, crab claw and John Dory
Fresh anchovies, fresh, oily sardines
Clothed in their crackling armour of batter.

The breeze off the sea is a cool, short-lived relief
The sea shimmers and wriggles its sequins
Like the *frizzante vino bianco* we drink

Sipping in pauses of silence, from the rising liquid
Thinking of the touch of stretching fingers
Across our bellies' and torsos welcoming flinch

The rub, *Il freggare* of flesh in an apricot afternoon
Of tawny light, the cool harbour of our room
Waiting upstairs with its panorama; shutters flung wide
   toward Vesuvius.

My Daisy Mae

'what will we do with ourselves, this afternoon…and then the day after that?' – Scott. F. Fitzgerald, *The Great Gatsby*

You were my Pepsi-Cola
I was your aspirin – but the angel
I first glimpsed, fizzed and floated away
As soon as I began to know you a little better…

In the story of how I lost my innocence
And you lost your patience with my poverty – and swept
Up your pearls, grey satin high heels – and headed for the stage exit –
For years we drifted further away on tailwinds of different destinies.

Yet in dreams I struggled to bring us back –
A big production with three acts; Passion, Longing and Regret;
You stand in your glowing bell of a gown at the end of the pier
I swim through the moonlit waves, splashing clearer
And nearer to love, just a roll and a twist ahead in the jealous mist.

Yesterday I was told your arranged marriage continues
On a tax-exile ship as you slowly criss-cross
Impoverished lassitudes and longitudes –
Walking the moonlit deck after bridge with an after-dinner mint
The lamplight rippling around your shining silver satin dress

And the ship's bells ringing chimes through islands of fog…
While here I still drive around, trying to be awesome and callous
Grinning at life from inside the door of my old Fleetwood Cadillac –
Instalments almost done; panels dinged but no rust
Humming along to the remnants of a popular song

We used to sing once; not always in harmony, but so much in love –
Cruising along, the soft top down and the lonely cicadas howling.

Nine lives

for Ann McGarrell

If I was a cat, I'd
Bring you a mouse
In thanks for taking care

Once upon a strange and wonderful time.

Oh how dispersed we all are
Scattered from our communal lamps
Hunched over our hearths of fire

Our nights and days raging with words
Windy discourses; phrases tightrope walkers.

Today in this orderly beautiful park
I walk and remember, Paris, Rome, Florence, Dublin
How many lives we lived then

How many lives I had to live
Down those streets of moonlit stones –
More than a cat, perched watching from its marble mantle.

Reunion at the remembered lake

Rowing onward in the early morning
I watch the wake undulating
Like your hair cascading backwards

I watch the drops from the oar blades
Falling and spinning away
Just like our thoughts condensing

And floating into a world of mist and air.
Today the willows trail leafless plaits
And are stooped and somehow morose
The conifers continue, glowing gold-combed totems, loners

And I sense in the pauses of autumn wind a drifting suspense
As you rhythmically lean forward and back and row
The rollicks making the familiar soft echo –

Your hair catches light again and again
Over your eyes, over your mouth
As you pull the oars back into your torso

And then let go, a terse smile with each release.
I know when we get to the shore
You will leave, not stay, hardly likely to return.

Too many memories this day to keep intact
Too many moments jarring from before
Which do not stop anything or help anymore.

The wind to come, is ruffling water
Is reckoning cold things, in the gliding pauses
Winter's claws brush across my cheek, a touch

To tell me; another signal to know of a terrible thing
And I am remembering the future already
As I see your imagined going, smiling hesitantly

While your warm breath, lingering, freezes across memory.

Rodin

You think of a woman like wine?
I'd rather chew something

Substantial – slowly, softly of course.
Poppies in wheat; swaying

Evidence for the times
We embraced in that field

Only summer left for clothes
Lips plum dark from country red

We made a cushion of yellow stalks, for our bed –

A raven blinking solemnly afterwards

Peering from an oak branch –
At our discarded bodies and cast off clothes.

The heavenly tie

'After the spirit of the moon' – Arthur Loureiro

She came in on the back of a tailwind, the gusty refractions
Of my dream, astride a slice of the new moon
Swooping through the massive door of my Russian ice palace
Through melodious resonances of blue

She leapt off her slice of lunar scooter, tossed it aside
And turned around on roller skates
Naked in all but dimples and a celestial blue tie
Tied in a Japanese knot around her waist

I remembered it from somewhere (Balthus maybe?)
But for the moment it was still unclear where
Beneath shimmers and shifts of memory –
I watched her move as she worked at her momentum

Turning a curvaceous figure of eight
Naked legs and arms blurring away across the icy space
In a slide slowing as her arms swung for pace
And traction and several zigzags of more acceleration

Her arms and thighs and slanting calves
Digging down through each curve
And the tie flew back behind her
A heavenly rail for those turns and twirls

Her body inclined above her pedalling motions
A shapely bow-sprite, her blue breasts pert
Above her stretching, contracting, arabesques
Then she smiled a blur of contrivance

And flipped twice, clicking hips and knees
And her heels in an arched trifecta and leapt into
A blue arc through portals of wavering translucence
And I woke just then – oh my god! – celestial tie twisted

Into a scrawny knot, fingers struggling with a collar
A carnation crushed in one fist
Pinstripes, handkerchief
Rollerskate marks, diagonals
Of whatever she did –
Dregs of a dank reality; and my rag doll head.

The swimmers

The pool where I watched unseen
Amongst the chorus of cicadas, while you swam
Thrusting naked, is still there in my dream, your lunges

Like fish pulses – undulating here and there
Head, arms and legs striving under water – a mirror of sequins
Rocking, flowing over a rippling foreground of my memory.

The rock where you sat to finger-comb your hair
Is still there, with the water set in rust and crimson forever
In a tide of estuarial memory, and then

The auburn island we swam toward afterwards –
Sinking into water on fire; again and again turning together naked
Languid fingers making silver circles over the surface; waits still there

Like the rock where you ducked down, bunching thighs, rose and dived
Splashed under, metres of wriggles away finally surfaced, laughing wildly –
Splashing sounds echoing – saying you will still remember.

Woman Cat

In thoughts, you hurled her
From the top of a wall
Shining swathe of hair, dress
Floating, bare toes curling

And like a cat she landed on all fantastic feet –
Not quite getting it, purring and her
Back arching, tail invisible hook
Tied to just another silly game.

Your memory scratches through a pen
Thinly – a thread of seething – convulsive
Again and again, you close your eyes
On her – hopefully a part of another world's noise;

Scratching darkness, dinging daylight
A waft, a fade of melody, but here
She comes through the dizziness
Of light – scampering back into your sight

Into the weariness of your eyes –
Cat woman bounding back into your life
The stage of autumn leaves a drifting vision
Memory thawing again, light captive, eyes resigned.

Tania

Take care of her
Dear lord
She is
My distant daughter.

In dawn's real silence
I hear her ocean whisper
I hear her river fall
Staircase of clear water.

Silence of years
That drowns all roars.

IV

Mongarlowe Country

A human weathervane

I've been on a horse
For days in this august wind
A weathervane, cantering across dark fields.
August is always the dying month
They say in the wind-strewn hills hereabouts.

The cows are lying down
Ready to calve, the foxes wait
Close, for the prized calf's tongue
Hanging loose, drooling for its mother's milk.

For the fox, an easy pate kept with one lunge…
I ride up and down the forest line
Scaring fox's eyes away
Saving tongues and mothers ready for lactation

But some will not escape –
A job as well done, I suppose
As any might be at four in the morning.
The tongues, apart from those in horrible dreams

May appear later, in some candle-lit place
Seasoned and salubriously served
On a glowing platter
With herb mustard or bechamel.
But that is a different matter
Another chapter, beyond the birthing of a calf.

Her coiled blue curves

He had loved the river from early days
And thought she had been misplaced
In the order of things; unsung, unpraised
Remaining little known all those years

With her sleek blues and her skipping silvers
Her way of curving under the gums and wider afterwards
   into the light
She swelled through, onward then past borders of the land he
   had inherited –
Like an unearthed waterfall, borrowing as much of the greens

Or blues as she needed – and he liked the way birds
Flew, gliding up and down her course
Using her waters as a beacon, her shining continuing
To amplify their cries – sent flying onward to feathered kin

Hidden in the gathered trees – or surprised stalking the grassy
   water's edge.
The river remained in his mind; a living leap, an arabesque
   swishing of silver
When he journeyed through the world – and he saw her
One night in the Seine's undulating reflections – and as a
   twist of silver

In the reddening sky above the Thames' greys and blues –
He saw her in the buildings floating in Manhattan waters
Rolling through the wavering shapes, the wobbling geometry –
He saw her in the Tiber, that seam of quicksilver triggering
   through the slow greens

Lazing under the parasol pines – in Piazza Navona he sipped his coffee
Missing her – in front of Bernini's rusting travertine rivers, sipping cool wine
Thinking of her supple greenness – at the end of the year
He returned, counting hours rippling southward over dusty bitumen

And running through the remembered paddock he reached the unprepared
River bank and squatting there beside her again, he did dare to mention
The rivers he had seen – but made little of it – and allowed her to flow about his
Offered hand, dipping carefully into her faithfulness, like the feelings

When a favourite cat brushed him, coiling its tail around his legs.
It was good to be back; to continue the tender talk of before –
She was his well-hoarded mistress, there was no doubt of this
And her beauty was best kept where it was, where now

She flowed on her own, under dusk or dawn skies – for him and no one else.

Southbound

My mother would begin
To pack up and
We knew we were on the move

Father driving, listening
Hourly to the news
The ABC a beacon

As we glided on through time
My mother feeding
Us Cadbury's milk chocolate

Content to watch the road
The concrete and the horizon
Widening always towards us

The bonnet swallowing time
As we drove the hours required
Our parents on a mission

We, behind, enjoying
The lark of another expedition
We had our own

Private jokes, we whispered them
Behind their stationary heads
Sometimes we would wrestle

Giggling or silent
To grapple with the boredom
But mostly we enjoyed

The spectacle of all worlds passing
The silences of the landscapes, closely coming, going
The sense of encapsulated

Movement, the hidden pact we had with time.
Today I drive on my own by satellite
Down the same silence of highway

The others have gone
To heaven, or estrangement
The same cantering hills

The same curve of dried lake
The same steep climb
Through scrub and stunted eucalyptus

The sudden rise, swooping toward
The storm's horizon, the silence
Under the rippled belly of the sky

And coasting down
At last the last descent
An avenue of dancing trees

Until I regain 'my destination'.
The end and the beginning
Of where I go to get to where I am.

The rock pool

Crouched down in the grass
You loved the way
The wind blew past
Too high to find you.

Or down by your favourite pool
In the creek where you waited –
Getting later for dinner, under
The arched branch of a reddening sky

The tadpoles forever, forever quivering –
Trembling to one place – until your father's urgent cry
Calling for you to hurry and come
And eat your dinner with mum

And him – facing the panes of the kitchen window
while you forked down steak, watching the way
The gum trees would shake in the wind, fascinated
By the way the crisp, swishing leaves

Tossed clumps of silver, back and forward again…
The keening cry of the crows, forging
Through red realms of sky, streaks of veering clouds
Left in long thumb strokes; the calm following the vanished wind.

Today you have grown but the feathered redness
Of a sunset is still clear evidence
Of those times, and you can still sense
Your old self back there; like a leaf or a curved blade of grass

Lying, tumbled into wilderness – but the witnesses
Of your childhood life; of your treks to the creek and back
Have gone, skies of swallows to somewhere else…
The proof of them continues to weather

In paired names, lichened into stone and their images
Sometimes seen in the vast quiet of clouds
Or floating half written in the wind, speared by cries of crows
And just over the rise, a congress of clouds
Still speaking memory, drifting higher into Clyde mountains.

A chair, best company?

Out there trees embrace dusk's
Crowding presence, clumps, shrubs, bushes
Swirls of cloaked leaves;
The squat shapes return – custodians

Of the half darkness; the trees welcome now
Arms uplifted to the moon's return
A golden silence
Curves with the flowing paddocks.

From the porch, slow stillness silences
The naturally planned world.
Across in the daylight
Of yesterday, cars move
Cutting through acres, pastures of innocence;

A toxic flow expelling the god of fumes;
A car mirroring my expression
Took you away, your
Resolve, your chuckling breasts

And one wonderful arse, all of your smile
Gearing up for the big smoke
No winding there, no curve vanishing
No flick or arabesque

Only the rigour of geometry –
The dour certitude of concrete –
Here I sit with my bachelor snake hips
An extra rib, a glass of red

And one rueful spoon

Tapping on pine – knots and grains of memories.
I will not shiver or despair
But the grass out there
Has decided, curving in droves

All the way west – following her rear end, through miles of darkness.

A cliff of sky between the birds

'The gene we have in common allows us to speak and for them to sing' – Margaret Atwood

The last of evening light leans far away
Endless all the way east, white trunks
And reaching branches of gum trees
Bathe in the light's long high tide.

Closer, slower, Lombardy poplars move ahead
Like glittering, spectral fountains, migrating across
The stubble of paddocks, pausing and continuing
Up along the hillcrests and over the undulating ridges.

The book I put down blurs chapters
In the dusk breeze, thoughts flicker – flutter
But do not settle; winter has lost its bite
The days are getting longer and blue-sky banks

Higher every evening, rising against the faltering light.
A molten mass of cloud hovers, burns like
A refrain of a bulging concerto
And crows drift like notes against the lingering fire.

In this hour you sit in one of your father's or maybe
Your mother's, interchangeable chairs
And sip your tepid tea and remember
On an earlier shadowed porch, how they ritually watched

The way the sunset and the ranked rows of forest trees
Played their game in diminishing light, all of this a subtle
Nuance of enjoyment, relished every evening – until the divorce –
Then the rules all changed and suddenly

All arrangements would never be the same.

My eleven-year-old mind saw them in another play –
As I imagined them like two huge ungainly birds, uncomfortable
Now with anyone's company, their unwieldy human wings
   grew suddenly
And they flew a short distance away; and they walked

Stiffly on the lawn keeping an eye on the porch
And toward me, conversing obliquely in their bird language
Seeming ready to migrate, to take off into the day beyond
Before finally vanishing where I could not see well enough to
   follow.

Years later, grown enough to finally get out of a boarding school
I remembered how the crow was entering their voices –
The hoarse croaks edging further out towards the sky
And how their posture changed; how they hunched tails
   down over

Their separate concerns; old certainties lost in awkwardness –
You sensed how they seemed to be abandoning things
Burying the outer layers, shedding their feathers and claws,
   beaks pointing
To newer eclipses, leaving their feathered personae

Like something ruptured and flung aside, souls inside-out
In two rumpled piles on the boards; each left behind a
   curving flight.

A friend, called mother

The number doesn't answer
It should be obvious
Its click disapproves
A room's silence reproves –
You know she's gone
And you're trying to get the dead
To lean over, pick up a Bakelite telephone!
No need either for mobiles when
Heaven is mobile; the clouds up there
Are portable turning loudspeakers

But her voice never makes an appearance.
You backstroke nostalgically remembering
Her joyously and mourningly; poets
Tend to drown in storms
Raging off Viareggio, she said –

Or dive, unable to swim, from bridges
In New Haven Academia – she was
A poet of thread, thimble and agile needle
Darning stitched your ongoing questions
Into rhythms and assonances. The rain
In grief, tapped several times at her window
But that same mother's smile surfaced to sustain
As she pulled and tightened the last knotted thread up.

Time slowly murdering her bowing face
Tired eyes attentive to the signalling needle
The ritual of repairing going on, whatever –
But that face still turns to me

At times above the wreckage of waves
As I swim further into cloaking mist and myth
Arm over arm, ploughing away
From penguin-suited or pinstriped sharks

Peering for orphans ahead; other
Children emerging, smiling – if befuddled –
Rescued from froth, from waves, from slowly drowning.

Acres of sunset

Veils of birds
Waft over the paddock
Seem to snag
On tendrils of a tree

Then shake out
Threads and dots of freedom
Flicker and whirl
Over the road

Following its gleam;
A shroud heading
Pulsing into the holocaust of the sun.
The highway's flame

Leaps for the mountains
A long golden kamikaze.

A single red rose

Rose – speaks of solitude
A single luscious note
Each petal composing
A fervent modesty;

Absence is red
Passion is red
Longing is
Wanting is, red.

Nothing brash about a rose
Demure in profundity –
Move an ear close
And what do you hear?

A heart folding over and over
Again – blurring down into innermost memory;
Red is remembering
Red is anguish
Red is flame enclosed

Red is plain delight, urge for a simple life.
An emperor kneels
In elegant regalia
To pluck you, a bloodied thumb now

To borrow your beauty
To conquer a queen;
As composed as a rose
Her solitude, stillness
Her poise proof, aloof for love.

Sky rider

Immense night sky
Immense her distances
Immense – her arching presence
Heart-warming outline against the starry sky –

It's hard to reach
And snatch a star, as to reach
And hold a heart, catch and hold a hand
Offered as she glides by – how long

Have I forgotten her?
More real, touchable now, than ever holding her
How long have I held her shadow
In my foolish arms? – my vagrant thinker's

Mad, oceanic, order – stars islands of my turning thoughts
Ravines of utter darkness undulate
Reefs of calmness high above, alternate, waves of memory – time between –
1 sail my soul like a dark hawk's wing;

A great sail, feathers spread full and dark
Keeling, tacking, furrowing across those waves
Riding rising swells against the star-cluttered sky
I remember well now – you were my star, my wave, and my wind
I followed and you whispered – yes, come, take me and sail me well.

Dawn bird

Through a lifting curtain of light
You call…the bird I know
But prefer to leave unnamed

Wanting instead to disembody
The sound you make
And more – if I could manage

To separate, uncreate the embodiment
Of such an exquisite thing
And let it float

An invisible fragment in its own free space –
like the cry of a special being
Just at this moment, uniquely born

It seeks a place, candid in the blue dawn
Unknown, unseen, but equal
Amongst the others who came before.

What I choose to do
Is simply aesthetic
A love for distilled, poignant stillness.

Others – creature of the otherness –
Would whittle you down
Pinning your liquid sound
To an image, a tag or a platitude.

You call again. I resist.
I will will the image
Of you – making the sound – further away.

I prefer the sole untouchable solitude
The immeasurable stillness
Filled with no feature

No distraction
To a single note
A song – singing to its own moment.

Dawn walk at Mongarlowe

Windswept undulations of land
Currents of cold air veering through pasture
Descending curves of virgin, brown furrows
All of this has no special significance
To a stranger's eye – but the clouded sky
Peering from darkening realms
Knows what I am doing and seeing
And the wind throwing wildflowers

Into a huddle, knows why I am going past here
Up and over one horizon, sketched grass curving
Walking down to another rim of sky – the birds in the trees
Black, white, crows, magpies and sulphur-tipped cockatoos
Send me fragments of music from leafless perches;
The score is spread along the bare branches of the morning
And the chords will change through the hours of the day
Moods of light and wind and birds circling, swooping to
　settle again –

Back in the view towards the house and the river
Autumn colours singing and sung through things
Mustards, golds in pencil-poplar fountains;
Burnt and riotous reds in towering maples;
Purples dripping in oaks like hovering grapes –

And the stubborn dust-green gums unchanging until their
　joyous leap into distant hills –

But I, the natural stranger here, the odd one; looking and sensing as much as I can –
Head from the last fenced paddock toward a rising assembly of ragged greens; light
Low under branches hosting the first illumination from sunrise –
Knowing where I am walking to – and as bird chatter erupts above me
I step after each shadowed step, striding over a well known mantle –
Toward the generations of lives, reflecting, imagining on my ancestor's –
My grandparents, my parent's striving, blooded time and efforts;
Spent, spread about; these rumpled dull ochres right under my path;

My soul knows, a listener and a whisperer underfoot.

I have no choice, as long as I am able
I will walk where I believe I belong, my shadow, shorter or longer
Knows the way, so does the sky, so does the turning day
It is not as if I am compelled to move in this way

I speak to myself, I know I have no choice
And on this at least, there is nothing more to say.

Fido

My Irish setter is funny sometimes
Pretending to be a folding
Table, on its side, with
One leg slack – hesitant.

Or famished for leaves
When they fly out of reach
Then happily gone gaga, tongue hanging out
Following the seagulls as they hop step and jump ahead.

She is very good at focusing on blowflies
For as long as they take to cross the room
A snap of the jaws on the thought
Of catching the elusive morsel, but then

She can be very serious; Shakespearian
At times, turning on the crest of a hill
In the last light of a sunset, bounding
Against the golden flow with her rhythmic explosions

Of red shaggy coat – impersonating the spirit of autumn –
But the trick with one ear perched and two wet eyes
Swinging toward the open door; yes, nod, and nod again –
Yes, wink, wink once more – she wouldn't say no, to another
  walk.

For whom?

Light – down through a cathedral
Of thought; a stillness of what is missing.
A bird sliding out of sight
The wave gone, spray in the air

Frozen there. Then sounds return
And the wind from the sea resumes
And the swells roll shoulders with curling glimpses
One second of a tumbling god? Then gone, you hear the slow
   monotone

Of the tide; to the east through spectral scaffolds
Of light, the palaces of the morning
Juggle, coordinate; clouds from a shoreless world
Glide by, bulky with silence; temples of no place.

Indian summer

I was late born
A common fly, I didn't know
The summer was over.

The leaves I was bred to expect
Were gone, the sun had fallen
Asleep across the forest floor.

There were other insects lost like me
So we danced, weightless
Drifting in wonderful currents of air –

Odd ones out, then intoxicated
With the vanishing swishing of moths
We followed as dots did into the auburn light.

But there was nothing ripe
Or pliant to land on; some clung
To twigs or spikes or even green needles

Others tried to hide, disguised
As parts of a rough thread of bark
Some thought it best to climb and retire

Into skeletal nests in sun-gilded branches –
Others buzzed before tumbling into burrows
Most didn't know the dance had already ended

Suddenly, as it had begun; as the dots gradually peeled off
I, too, finally let go and floated into the ribbons
Of crisp air, into the unfairness of homeless cold
Into the sheen of snow glare, into the glow of ending.

Mother again

Mother shuffling from a gateless nightmare
The fence gone awry the cows run out
The moon not quite where it ought to be –
Never complain never explain
She would mutter into her sleeplessness

Even in dreams not just daylight
She had to keep silence
Like the girl who instead
Of reading a book after school
Had to do something useful.

Out of the yard crossing the pasture
Got to do something useful
Mutterings escaping on the way to school
Wearing aunties' jacket sleeves remade for pants
Barefoot because the eldest brother

Could not be seen getting about without good shoes.
Hiding bare, nut-brown feet under her satchel
Away from the teachers ruthless eye –
Feeling her way down corridors
Away from the fenceless, gateless dream

Counting the doorknobs, everything there
Now around the corner getting away
From teachers, nurses, fathers, uncles
Getting ahead of husbands, accountants
Collectors of taxes and vengeance

Still one more lawyer to go, the corridor
Going through to the paddock now
Toward the golden moon – black Angus cattle
Drifting left or right, with one mind;
A collective, masticating windvane – but

No time to be distracted got to be useful
Whatever I do, edging along the ridge
Above the sheep station, using the cry of the dingo
As a guide, heading toward the veranda in the sky
Moon-brushed, the whirring windmill hums

Blades pumping earth into water – magic, isn't it?
Blades slicing through wind and rare rain
Turning through a girl's sleep, turning against
The zigzags of lightning, turning like a wheel
Following after a young girl's life, bouncing then, far into the
   night.

Nature sinuous with her maker

Art is the stealthy one
An intruder here I think –
In this moment it might be a glimmer
A sunburst through green – a blur sluggish
Over slate, flesh or clay, or a leaf
Trying to fall forever while others
Are spinning in light; might it be
A hand returning, dappled to a lap?

It's confessing it's here in things;
Shines, dulls, hints – reminds sometimes.
You want to remember before the others arrive
An inner voice pleads, please
Do not come into this garden – burdened by dramas
Of high-rise life, your strings of ping-pong talk –
Your chronically unhappy dog –

Try a rest before you return on your way.
From this bench, this rickety table with a glass of wine
You will enjoy the late flow of changing colours
Warmth in nature maturing; sweet or even bitter – one
Of life's memories may be hidden in this lemon – look – I will bite
Stinging through to heartbreak, or to halves; divided smiles –
Or better into love, soured though it might be.

Here in shade and light a wordless show goes on
Slowly outlines and colours criss-cross, rediscover
Each other; camouflage flows and goes
A newcomer shrub blows her flimsy green clothes –
A breeze discloses, encloses; wind the foliage's invisible gossiper.
Sunlight drips through openings high over
Trickles through leaves scissoring down to darkness, shifting –

Like unsettled dregs across entanglements of things –
The village man here says, an apple is happier, crisper
Bitten in pauses; brusque cuts to thought, let go or maybe kept.
Shadows grow, indifferent still but slowly entrancing greens
Across this garden; nature appears to love to mimic her
    persuader Artifice –
Other elements here, shrubs, orange trees, even my mottled
    arms, knees, fingers
My freckled skin just one more surface amongst grass, earth,
    and pebbles –
A patchwork of living things; natural patterns shifting over
    memory.
Several cypress trees close by, circle a marble Venus, guardians
Of her head's absence, consolers of her missing right arm –

I squat here in my shadow – agitated
Witness to her incomplete loveliness;
Curves of shade draped over her belly and thighs;
Probably better to ruminate, not reply
With ill-fitting ideas – to the quietness of evocative beauty.

The dozing rhythm goes on
Sunshine forages in the uppermost leaves
Floods again through branches
Trickles of gold, arteries of sunlight
Molten moments thinned into darkness.
And far away with a glowing skin
The lake glistens her brief moods –
Warbling small birds and gliding predators
Higher overhead remind me – I am also guest

For a long moment, in nature's kingdom –
But restless now, I will go – rolling up my sleeves
Taking up the oars, lunging ahead with a thought
In my hopeless craft – rowing finally
Away from mankind's artifice –
Classic facsimiles, fidgety guests, ornate memories and my silly self
Blades scooping, rising, spray flying, oarlocks echoing
Back aching, new desire swaying eagerly, toward inscrutable wilderness.

Not taken

The plane tree leaf
Spun down and touched
My head as it fell into the snow
And lay there animate with its little

Leaf ends like upturned claws
Trying to be noticed.
A leaf that fell on my head
The Italians once told me was good luck

It was too brittle to put in my pocket
To portentous to crush, by error
Or intent – I carried it by its stem
As I went on the usual route of my walk

Along by the edge of the forest where in mist
The trees seemed to have come further to meet me
Past the gate where I once stopped but did not go on in
Around the edge of the lake all white and golden

Following the old path flooded by the moon
Sketched along through frozen grass
That took me back home a long time ago
When I almost walked on into that cold white world –

Making a decision not to give up
To continue to live
And care for the things
That needed me to continue to live

Following the thin worn whispering line
In the snow, crisp steps in the mind
Blurring back to the windows, hanging like
Lanterns, and a door waiting

In the waiting whiteness
For me to show up, coming home.

Omelette?

Hard to beat innocuous eggs
Already sad to break two shells
But then to whip the insides
Into submission; a yellow

Coagulated shape is worse again –
Watching thoughts shrinking into a form
Folding rigor mortis, falling over onto a plate
A rug sliding, hiding an uncooked soul.

One bird

Things are so still
On certain days
It's like forever
Not just entranced air;
The windlessness of existence

But the buildings
The shed, the cottage, the barn
Proceed – at a halt – like ships becalmed
Anchored on meticulous pasture
Memory that does not tick over

For some time, silence
Moored with a cloud to a tree –
Only one bird needed
To set it free; a shocked crow
Jammed in the sky.

Playful thinking

A thought that bounces
When we fumble and drop it –
Floats back up into my hands
That's what I want
Instead of chasing a figure, through fairgrounds of mirrors –

Or into a lane of leaning shadows.
I want to put on a thought
Like a season's new set of clothes
And walk through a spring or an autumn
And see how it fits the turning cycle –

Follows the years of sky. How can you think
Of something and then it flits
Away, just like a butterfly?
See! How pretty – look – the rhythmic dips and rises
But then it's gone; just the dust of its wings, on my fingers

The last cull on the place

General disarray…random stone and brick rubble, scatterings left
Of metal offcuts, the disembowelled tractor tyres
Rusted axles, iron-rimmed wheels missing spokes, buckets now colanders

Point a track to decline. Time has collided hard –
A sharp swipe, an uppercut
To a life. This scrawl of farm junk like

A farewell gesture hung out in breaths of silence –

Once useful implements, oiled bits and pieces of metal;
A trail of objects that seem to have lost direction and stopped
Across the yard of once, hammered and forged, orderly repair.

A red sheepdog pauses by a rusted wall, shadows are silent
Across corrugations; a slow eery creaking, the dog seems to listen intently.

2

At the back door on the porch, sunlight pulses
In shorter bands along the wall, as if
Having searched for a person, a grown up, a teenager or a newborn child

To touch with warmth – just to find one soul to colour with light –
It seems now to have given up and pours exhausted into one pool.
An echo of the shot is heard again in the buckling of the roof iron

Corrugations wheezing and easing when the breeze lifts
Rippling its fingers along under the western gable of the house.
The sky is dispersed in streaks of clouds, a great arch of dusk-brown –

Vertebrae of cumulus seem to be frozen, twisted in shock…

3

The shot echoes again, a whine in the expanse of ochre land –
Over the red curve that leads toward a listless windmill
The last steady heartbeat of the pump has gone, suddenly a
 banging –

The pounding of the horses escaping – hooves
Crashing out from the shattered planks of the yard's fence
Is echoed in a broken exodus of clouds, stretched

Low down, hovering far out on the horizon
Where the fence line lies slack or bounds in coils of rusty
 lengths of wire.
Rust is the dominating colour now, in the browns

That bleed along with shadows, slow from porch to outhouse
From barn to blacksmith's shed, to the solitary, prim
Weatherboard dunny, set at a respectable distance from the
 house.

4

And along the porch to the western corner, are those loose
Pages of a life; a testimony of blown paper – accounts, invoices
Fees and sheets of bank interest, amounts mostly unpaid

Stir in the wind's breath and fall and settle again on the boards…
A litter of unforgiving, leading to the banging fly-screen door
And the rocking chair with the body slumped

Into a rumpled form; folds and scraps
Of loose-fitting clothes, weathered browns and faded
Overcoat, a dumped blanket trying to come to life.

5

The flies' noise becoming louder now
As a drone of separate intensity, urging
The drained presence, the slumped absence, to get up and go,
    but it doesn't.

The head lolled, the 12-gauge shotgun fallen close beside
The mouth torn into a bigger orifice
And the flyscreen clicks and swings and slams

And bangs a kind of Morse code that cannot leap far enough
To get to a wire to travel over and so continually short circuits
Into the view; a distance of fields gone grey and no rains that
    came in time.

The man without leaves

i.m. Mark Strand

The beech tree reaches high
Into the middle of grey winter sky
Bare tips stretch toward the paused clouds –
Throwing a bouquet of white branches

A fractured fresco – up against solemn sky.

White filaments flaring like
Remembered fireworks, like an idea
Photographed, a negative, frozen in the mind…
Below the tree is the same naked man again, standing there

Head thrown back looking up a trunk rising upward to light

His outstretched arms held in sympathy with criss-crossing tendrils
The drifting gaps of blues and whites, fingers spread
In communion with the earth and sky –
The shaggy white dog panting beside him looks

At the man's fingers fluttering, and knows already
The man is thinking up a poem called – fine tree alone in winter –
And his bare arms swing wide, as he turns around and around
And the dog sees again the naked man has lost

Every single one of his leaves…
But remembers it would be normal at this time of the year
And the icy marsh lying around the man and tree
Is simply a mirror surrounding a lonely being's heart…

The dog has watched, waiting for him to thaw all these years
And now he watches again as the man's arms rise
To brace and lift the weight of a questioning white sky

To hold back a mass of whiteness in the sky
Which will not resolve itself and will not roll or glide either –
Nothing will come to the earth now, nothing will be released in drops

Or flakes, or even hail, nothing given in warmth or raining comfort…

And spring watches everything, from an unthawing peak
Knows some of her tears, frozen down there
Are stored in the heart of that man –
A man leaning, intent, into a cold wind – with no more leaves to spare.

The marathon

The pants have not reached
The other side of the room yet –
But the configuration tells
You they will get there soon

Enough – one sock, underpants, a wallet
May not; the shirt thrown over
The shoulder of a chair has not given up
But pauses there before more action.

And you? Who threw you into the bed?
Submerged between a storm of sheets
What great current does your arm cross?
The other limp, coasting behind? With one sock left

You swim the channel, amazing public
And gathering waves and gulls – some
Who placed their eager money
On the pants, now seek better odds –

For the sock there is just not a lot of leeway
And those that punted on the shirt
Are dismayed; revealed as prone to taking naps
Close to the finish, its casual *savoir faire*, slackened;

Arms hanging, cuffs unbuttoned, signalling retirement.

The mountains watch

You may ask why I am standing here
Found in what seems to be nowhere
But from this higher ground, above
The pasture of my forefathers

Turned with the forest descending at my back –
I know these mountains will be watching me;
Squinting – such blue peaks of scrutiny –
While I take in with my gaze

The lazy river; lush grass flowing along beside her
The rolling hilltops and sun-struck ridges – like old friends
Intent and yet affectionately disregarding me
Their long look warm on my shoulder blades.

I ignore their faint disapproval
Confess I have wandered and have spent
My tinkling silver; my brightest coins of that time
On other shores, slopes, villages, below different mountains

For I have been the discordant one
And called a fool to have gone so far
And hopefully a smarter fool by far –
I returned because finally I knew no stronger love

Than this land could give quietly back to me.

The river below runs from all places deep
Before now and will for centuries' seasons after this day –
Its melody before, and here, resonates
Like booms of distant places recurring in a cave

The river twists its toiling waters into me
Reproves me for those rivers I swam and laughed in, far away –
I hear my life cascading back like
A waterfall that jumped its usual course

I changed my mind and turned right over
Diving back into the lap of my motherland;

This dry and lush terrain, this sudden sunlit land
This place of windswept loneliness
This place of little joyous, lamp-lit bays
This land of indifferent pinnacles of cities

This horizon of outstretched, expectant emptiness
This outback of the solitary yellow dog's catastrophic cry
This country of flares of reds and yellows –
Sunsets slung in tides around old mountains;

This place I dreamt about by the shores of Ligurian villages –
By the ruins of ancient Tiber peoples – yes, tonight I listen to
   this river

Her slow murmuring, her restless, nurtured secrets –
While remembering mountains, moon-painted over
   Mediterranean seas
Those legendary seas of sirens, sailors, writers of journeys
And to the sound of this last river in my life, I begin to write

A scratch down on a page or two; rustling a quiet salute
To those rivers, which brought me back

To their humble sister; this river still today unwritten
But singing for dawns and sweeping dusks of time
Murmuring music to glide and rush with her youthful song
And always singing the next beginning; a daybreak song

Tumbling, following on forever – alongside her unsung self.

The old place

Time runs away in stars
Across the windshield glass
Racing against the dark

Streaming past
As quick as it comes, the wind
Will smooth away

The random lashings of rain –
The grass curves goodbyes in a wake behind.

As you step out of the car
Memory cloaks you in a blur
Night birds you remember, some announcing your return.

The moon hesitates, baulks to offer a mellow word
While steps you make toward the porch
Seem to be foretold, you walk in an airless

World where even your own breathing
Seems remote, two steps, and then a stumble, after
Floating up to the boards, the door, it's still unlocked…

The polished planks of the corridor
Creak along toward a steady glow, you know
Black Labrador dogs, illuminated by the fire

Are asleep just out of sight; around
The flickering corner, winged armchairs
And a lumpy Victorian couch, all wait for sure

With a famous painting done of the same room
Brush strokes melted by tongues of a glowing lamp
The mantelpiece clock will tell the same time

Above the floating specks of fire –
Suddenly deep bongs of the hall clock, ticking
Tocking out of the frame of the mirror that gilded your
    parents' faces

Striking just before you turn…turn the corridor –
Corridor…to confront an empty room, room…
Hushed by the smell of must; ashes stirring
Embers dead, smoke curled forever in the fireplace.

Those moments

When I want
To watch
Gods
I become a bough
In the gilded forest.
When I want
To hear and see
Silence
I go into a huddle of stone.

In the grove
Probed
By light and dark
I become
Chiaroscuro
Now

My thoughts
Are like moth's wings
Caught in a curtain –
Hopelessly I struggle
One lunge at a time –
Trapped in a life
But in a few releases
Briefly divine.

Peninsula

You think it's an illusion
When islands appear
To move, souls lost
In seas of fog

When autumn furrows turn and hide
In the longer nights
When trees plead their plight
Of nakedness and rabbits and birds

Seem baffled without those leaves to hide.
Winter will want even more
Granting no illusions, no regrets
In the strict stillness, in a cold gifted

To us like penitence. But you, a furrow
Of sorts, will walk the winter out
Learning again to love the browns
To love the gulls' even lonelier cry

Until spring creeps shamefacedly
Then brazenly back, regaining lost acres
Trickling her greens of hope and return
And the islands and the higher forests

Will be on the move again
Cloaked in leaves
Of offspring
Ready for anything.

Washing up

The kitchen a startled museum
Dishrag hung like a dried bat
Plates in the rack; a doomed platoon –
A fly negotiates a Venetian ladder

Of light, slanting to a detergent bottle
Super concentrate remarks on the silence
And her breathless apron; duty limp from a nail.
She had said, carefully putting

Clean glasses up into a cupboard;
'It's twenty-five years, I've eaten
Here on my own'; those years
Are gathered in this squared-off

Order; taps turned so tight to confirm
Her thoughts; every night draining
Out of the stainless steel sink;
A life of reminders to do or not to do

And a fly circumspectly confirms it all.

Will I?

Will I one day
Become the old place
With newspapers flattened
Against the inside of my windows?

Will I be one crack left of light
Squinting out into the night?
Could I one day tick like rusted iron
Or the buckled mudguard in the backyard?

Will I one day be filled with the constant
Hum of blowflies; the spawn of my untruths laid
Down corridors and rooms, hatching before my spectral eyes?

Will I one day become the loosened gable
That wheezes up and down in the prising wind
Or whistles through the creaking silence
Of my innards? Will I become an audience

Of sedate furniture, posed, expectant
In perpetual light, or an armchair
Placed beneath an unwound clock –
Trying to work out when it's time to move?

Will I one day become
The walls that fall – suddenly –
Pushed inward by too many pendulums of the sun
Light bearing down and leaden rain;
The tin roof hammered thinner, under
The gathering winds of memories;
The wild momentum of clouds and skies.

Towards another summer

There is a newborn calf dead by the yards
Its tongue taken at first light by a fox
A life swiped for a tongue, what an exchange –
Need is swift and ruthless in nature.

In days then weeks which pass while
September wind sways in the creaking conifers
The fallen shape is stripped to sketched white bone –
Life, like the maggots, feeds fervently from death to survive;
And a year unravels its mosaics of circling patterns

New light and older darkness renewing
Erasing and replacing a brace of seasons
Stepping forwards, then into place – until it's spring again
And as if nothing had happened –

We see a crow perched for a wing-beating moment

On the coiled ribs of last spring's death –
The calf's skull, perfect, pristine, cushioned by daisies
And a mound of clover; ants crawling through eye sockets
Have carried away a hundred times their number and strength

And the mother has given birth to another calf
That bleats and butts and punishes up under her udder
Bellowing before it finally gets its grip on the teats
Tugs down and sucks for its right to life, under skies shifting

Constantly onwards, sailing toward loftier cathedrals of light –
And the single death of last spring is taken for granted
Blurred in torrents of luscious pasture and swinging yellow
 buttercups
While slants of summer fall; golden blessings across the
 emigration of grasses.

Acknowledgements

Poems in this collection have appeared in the following:
Five Bells, Henry Kendall/Central Coast anthologies,
Overland, *Quadrant*, *Canberra Times* and Fairfax Media, *The Irish Independent*, *Westmeath Independent*, *Canberra Poets* anthology, *Australian Love Poems* anthology, Irish Centre for Poetry Studies anthology, Poets In Cahoots anthologies (Dublin), Sigh Press anthologies (Florence), Contrappasso anthologies (Sydney).

www.ingramcontent.com/pod-product-compliance
Lightning Source LLC
Chambersburg PA
CBHW071814080526
44589CB00012B/795